THE
TRAGIC MIND

Fear, Fate, and
the Burden of Power

Robert D. Kaplan

Yale

UNIVERSITY PRESS

NEW HAVEN AND LONDON

Published with assistance from the Mary Cady Tew Memorial Fund.

Yale University Press books may be purchased in quantity
for educational, business, or promotional use. For information, please e-mail
sales.press@yale.edu (U.S. office) or sales@yaleup.co.uk (U.K. office).

Set in Yale and Gothic type by IDS Infotech, Ltd.
Printed in the United States of America.

Library of Congress Control Number: 2022936311
ISBN 978-0-300-26386-2 (hardcover : alk. paper)
ISBN 978-0-300-27677-0 (paperback)

A catalogue record for this book is available from the British Library.

10 9 8 7 6 5 4 3 2 1

To Jim Thomas

Ah, the frailty of joy. . . . We are none of us safe.

—E. M. FORSTER, *The Longest Journey*, 1907

Fear saves us from so many things.

—GRAHAM GREENE, *A Burnt-Out Case*, 1960

CONTENTS

CONTENTS

PREFACE

I spent my formative years in the 1980s as a foreign correspondent covering communist Eastern Europe, the Greater Middle East, and Africa while based in Greece. My interest in the ancient Greeks and their influence on Shakespeare and modern literature was kindled in Athens, from where I traveled constantly to see the very things the Greeks feared: chaos and forms of order so extreme that they were, in fact, species of chaos.

Nothing I experienced was more terrifying than Saddam Hussein's Iraq. Iraq then was one vast prison yard lit by high-wattage lamps. It constituted a level of tyranny worse than even Hafez al-Assad's regime next door in Syria, which I also knew from reporting trips. The only place to which I could compare Saddam's Iraq was Nicolae Ceausescu's Romania, yet another part of my beat. At one point in the summer of 1986, Iraqi security police confiscated my American passport and I was left in limbo, living with Kurdish militias in the north for ten days. Despite all the other horrors I had experienced around the world, Saddam's Iraq, with its massive billboard pictures of the dictator everywhere, its multiple intelligence services, its reputation for torture on almost an industrial scale, and its cowering diplomats in Western embassies who told visitors they could do nothing for them if the regime found them suspicious, registered an unequaled level of fear. I remember alienating, monumental architecture like dragon's teeth breaking into the Baghdad sky, celebrating the greatness of the dictator. The intimation of violence was as suffocating as the heat and dust outside the long, machine-gun-guarded walls of the presidential palace. All this led me, in the wake of 9/11, to support the Iraq War, despite my worries about what could befall Iraq in a post-Saddam era.

I was a journalist who had gotten too close to my story. I had let my emotions overtake dispassionate analysis. My moment of comprehension came when I returned to Iraq embedded with U.S. Marines during the first battle of Fallujah, in April 2004. There I experienced something far worse than even the Iraq of the 1980s: the bloody anarchy of all against all that Saddam's regime, through the most extreme brutality, had managed to suppress. The clinical depression I suffered for years afterward because of my mistake about the Iraq War led me to write this book. I had failed my test as a realist — on the greatest issue of our time, no less! What would henceforth ring in my ears was the observation of the medieval Persian philosopher Abu Hamid al-Ghazali, that one year of anarchy is worse than a hundred years of tyranny.[1]

Over my four-decade career as a foreign correspondent I have been consistently terrified by the deadly, themeless violence that I saw at close range, not only in Iraq but in Yemen, Afghanistan, Sierra Leone, and elsewhere. I also witnessed tyranny at such extreme levels — particularly in Stalinist Romania and Baathist Iraq, where literally anyone could be arrested, tortured, or killed for no reason — that I came over time to understand it as anarchy masquerading as order.

Anarchy was the ancient Greeks' greatest, most fundamental fear. The Greeks were too rational to ignore the power of the irrational that lay on the other side of civilization. They saw no moral equivalency between order and disorder. In Greek tragedy, an orderly universe – the opposite of chaos – is always a virtue. The modern world lost this sensibility amid the monstrous perversions of order imposed by Hitler and Stalin, which helped inspire the dystopian fiction of Aldous Huxley's *Brave New World* (1932) and George Orwell's *1984* (1949) – two books that featured regimes so chilling that they gave order itself a bad name.

Of course, once order is imposed, the task is to make it less and less tyrannical. The Founders of the American Revolution grappled with this issue and had fierce debates over it. That order has no substitute, and yet also carries grave dangers, is one reason the Greeks saw the world as deeply imperfect and yet beautiful.

The Greeks found great value in learning how to fear chaos and thus avoid it. Fear warns of so many things. For there is much that we *don't* know about what can befall us as a nation, and as individuals. Sophocles' *Oedipus the King* teaches that no man can be judged as fortunate until he is dead – since nothing is certain and therefore nothing can be taken for granted. The same is true of a nation. The wisest among us are full of fear, which is future-oriented. This is especially true of those in power, who decide about war and peace. Wise leaders are those who know that they must think tragically in order to avoid tragedy. Vladimir Putin never learned this lesson or else he never would have invaded Ukraine.

Greek tragedy emerges out of the need for constructive fear, or anxious foresight, and goes on to encompass much else. For example, true tragedy is characterized by a searing awareness of the narrow choices we face, however vast the landscape. This is the world of constraints. To be self-aware is to understand, in any given situation, what is possible and what is not. Such self-awareness often comes too late to affect the outcome. The pathos and paradox of someone in high office is that despite having authority, the options he or she possesses can be truly awful.

Tragedy also insists that there is nothing more beautiful in this world than the individual's struggle against long odds, even as death awaits him, with little or no chance of being long remembered. This marks the true grandeur of the human spirit, since struggle always has a purpose and a chance of success. Tragedy is not fatalism; nor is it related to the quietism of the Stoics. It is comprehension: the comprehension and self-knowledge that I finally acquired in Fallujah when I realized how wrong I had been about Iraq, and why. But when one thinks tragically from the outset, one always fears the future and is therefore aware of one's limitations, and thus can act with more effectiveness. My aim here is to inspire, not to depress.

Greek tragedy, moreover, is not about common misfortune; nor is it about immeasurably vile crimes against humanity. Nicolae Ceausescu and Saddam Hussein, the two monsters of my early years as a foreign correspondent, could never be tragic heroes because they lacked the means to acquire self-knowledge. The tragic hero eventually finds wisdom. As the Greeks defined it, tragedy is not the triumph of evil over good but the triumph of one good over another good that causes suffering. Removing Saddam Hussein was a good thing, but it supplanted a greater good: the semblance of order. Even Saddam's lawless authoritarian rule was not the worst chaos that could befall his country; without him, hundreds of thousands in Iraq went on to die violently. Tragedy is about morally defensible but incompatible goals, since the choice of good over evil is too easy. Thus I have largely written evil out of this book.

Iraq was a failure of almost literary dimensions not because of evil, but because our leaders lost the ability to think tragically following the end of the Cold War. It is that sensibility that I seek to recover.

———

THE TRAGIC MIND

Chapter 1

THE BATTLE OF GOOD AGAINST GOOD

Forty years as a foreign correspondent have taught me that while an understanding of world events begins with maps, it ends with Shakespeare. Maps provide the context for events and the vast backdrop on which they are acted out. But the sensibility required for understanding those events — the crucial insight into the passions and instincts of political leaders — is Shakespearean.

Geography is required for the study of culture and civilization, which constitute the accumulated experiences of different peoples inhabiting particular landscapes for hundreds if not thousands of years. That cultural traits and tendencies cannot easily be quantified by contemporary political science does not reduce their importance. The map, in other words, is the foundation of all knowledge. I have lived with maps all my working life. They were the first things I consulted before flying to a foreign country on assignment. Maps spoke of both opportunities and limitations: some countries had coastlines and some did not; some were alongside the great sea lines of communication and many more weren't; some had mountain ranges that divided tribes and ethnic groups, many did not; some countries had good soils, while others did not; and so on.

And yet the map by itself is too fatalistic — the reason why the field of geopolitics, studied in isolation, yields up truths of only lesser interest. The truths of greater interest always involve the province of the heart, in which we drill downward from the map, to culture and accumulated historical experience, to finally the individual.

Men and women are not particles in a test tube whose behavior follows the laws of chemistry and physics. There is no hard, predictive science of international politics. There is only insight, which can be improved by the study of geography on one hand and the study of literature on the other, with a greater emphasis on the latter as one gets older. Historians grasp this. The best historians (and the best old-school foreign correspondents I have known) inhabit the exalted dimension of novelists. They know that within grand, determinative patterns, there is the impossible-to-predict chaos of human interactions, driven by disfiguring whirlwinds of passion and agency — so that great events can turn on a single gesture, or on a single offhand remark at a summit meeting that reveals a political leader's character even as it circles back to deep structural forces that historians and political scientists can study.

There is no geography as vast and as full of wonders and possibilities as the mind of Hamlet. Merely by thinking out loud, Hamlet breaks down cultural divisions and manifests a universalism that triumphs over geography.[1] Geography is magnitude, scale; Hamlet is particularity, minuteness. In literature, we call something an "epic" if it incorporates both elements.[2] Tolstoy's *War and Peace* and Carlyle's *The French Revolution* are two examples of immense and overpowering canvases, which nevertheless encompass the needle-point precision of individuals seeking to determine their own fates.

Yet something even more fundamental unites geography and Shakespeare: something that distills the drama of all these interacting elements — the map, civilizations, history, and individuals — and which thus regulates the greatest of literary epics, no matter how wide their scope. That something is tragedy, within whose confines operate all of literature, human nature, and world events. Tragedy begins with the searing awareness of the narrow choices we face, however vast the landscape: the knowledge that not everything is possible, regardless of the conditions. This is the world of constraints, both human and physical. To be self-aware is to understand what, realistically, is possible and not possible in any given situation. And such self-awareness often comes too late to affect the outcome. As Herodotus quotes the Persian: "we follow in the bondage of Necessity. This is the bitterest pain to human beings: to know much and control nothing."[3] Nevertheless, we have no alternative but to forge on. Analysis is the process by which we make difficult choices.

All this is only about what we *do* know. There is much that we don't know, and cannot know. Many times when a leader of a powerful country makes a decision to launch a military attack, despite all the intelligence assessments on his or her desk, he or she is operating inside a fog of uncertainty about the intentions of the country's adversaries. Vladimir Putin was operating blind on the eve of his invasion of Ukraine, the fog especially thick because of subordinates who feared an honest discussion with him.

Sophocles' *Oedipus the King* teaches that no man can be judged as fortunate until he is dead — since nothing is certain and therefore nothing can be taken for granted. Catastrophe can strike the most successful and powerful person at any moment, reducing the most charmed and privileged life to ashes. Because there is such a thing as fate — what the Greeks called *moira*, "the dealer-out of portions" — we require anxious foresight to guard against hubris.[4] That is, we must attempt to think tragically in order to avoid tragedy. It is only through anxious foresight – the knowledge that our circumstances can always change dramatically, and for the worse – that we learn modesty and are delivered from illusion. This is why vain and arrogant people are also foolish people. Tragedy, as the philosopher Arthur Schopenhauer tells us, exposes "the vanity of all human striving."[5] Tragic thinking, which internalizes this realization, means the discovery of self before you are forced to learn the hard truth about yourself in a crisis. The consummate Oxford classicist of the early and mid-twentieth century, Sir Maurice Bowra, once observed that the ancient Greeks knew human greatness is most apparent in disaster rather than in triumph.[6] Which is why they merged the heroic ideal with the tragic one.

Tragedy is about much more than grief. It is not about the triumph of evil over good: rather, it is about the exalted striving against insurmountable forces that leads to a new awareness about our lives and sanctifies human existence. As I've said, in writing about tragedy in international relations, my aim is to inspire, not to depress.

The word *tragoidia* (from *tragos*, or "goat") may have originated from the fact that the chorus in many Greek plays were dressed in goatskins, or like goats. Nietzsche, echoing Friedrich Schiller, writes that the chorus itself is the foundation of Greek tragedy, as it exists on stage as a "living wall . . . to shut out the real world and to protect its ideal ground."[7] This aligns with Hegel's insight that Greek tragedy is synonymous with both the anarchy and the splendor of the Heroic Age, when men were thrown back on their own resources because there were no institutional structures of state to protect them.[8] None of this should sound ironic or contradictory. As we shall see, there is nothing necessarily negative or even disheartening about thinking tragically.

———

Tragedy is central to why the Greeks were great – and thus central to the invention of the West. The same civilization that invented the tragic mind also defeated the Persian empire. Tragedy, which is the basis of self-awareness and signifies the loss of illusion, is organic to the development of individuality, which first manifested itself in classical Greece and led ultimately to the emergence of Western democracy.

The great American classicist Edith Hamilton, writing in 1930, explained that tragedy is the beauty of intolerable truths, and that (as I've noted earlier, and as Hegel had indicated in his *Philosophy of Right*) real tragedy is not the triumph of evil over good but the suffering caused by the triumph of one good over another good – and of one ethical person over another ethical person.[9] Tragedy was born when the ancient Greeks realized that there is "something irremediably wrong in the world," while such a world must be judged "at the same time as beautiful." "The great tragic artists of the world are four," Hamilton declared (again echoing Hegel), "and three of them are Greek": Aeschylus, Sophocles, and Euripides. The fourth, of course, was Shakespeare.[10] Precisely because Periclean Athens and Elizabethan England were periods of "unfathomable possibilities" – and not periods of "darkness and defeat" – the idea of tragedy could flourish. Those audiences, separated by over 2,000 years, were awestruck by the heroic and often futile struggles against fate, even as they were in a position – owing to their good and yet unstable fortune – to accept it with serenity. (Remember that the greatest tragedy of them all, Sophocles' *Oedipus,* was written at the very height of Athenian power under Pericles.) To be clear, tragedy is not cruelty or misery per se. Normal misfortune is only superficially and loosely tragic, since misfortune, as Schopenhauer tells us, "in general is the rule" of life.[11] The Holocaust and the Rwandan genocide were not tragedies: they were vast and vile crimes. They were not about the struggle of one good against another good, the telling of which uplifts us spiritually, but merely great evils. "The dignity and the significance of human life — of these, and of these alone, tragedy will never let go," Hamilton observes. Thus the tragic sensibility is neither pessimistic nor cynical: rather, it has more in common with bravery and supreme passion. Failure to think tragically is "sordid," she writes, since it robs life of significance.[12]

Because the ancient Greeks could see the world clearly, they had no trouble reconciling opposites. The Cambridge classicist F. L. Lucas, a contemporary of Bowra, wrote that "western tragedy" had at its birth "the magnificence, yet unhappiness, of man."[13] While the Greeks accepted injustice and horrifying fates as altogether natural, they also could feel at the most profound level the world's anguish. Euripides, for example, was a rebel and fighter against human suffering, relentlessly upholding the sanctity of the individual. Humanitarianism does not begin only with the Hebrew prophet Isaiah, but also with Euripides. This ultimately explains the mysterious power of humanitarian writing today. To rail repeatedly against inaction in the face of great violence and injustice, to do so even when the chances of having your pleas heard and acted upon by policymakers are slim, and even when a national interest in undertaking such a humanitarian action is hard to discern, still gains a large and appreciative audience. Realists, who emphasize the amoral interests of state, react to the public tribute paid to humanitarians with annoyance and bewilderment. But they should not be surprised or offended. They need only read or attend a performance of Euripides' *The Trojan Women,* and experience the pleasure that audiences for more than 2,400 years have derived from this tragedy about the sufferings of civilians in war, in order to comprehend the tragic sensibility at work. As human beings we are moved by learning about great injustice, even as we may be able to do little about it, and we even take a kind of pleasure in our own reaction. (To know what I mean, just listen to the "Chorus of the Hebrew Slaves" in Verdi's *Nabucco.*) This is not hypocrisy but an ambition toward a higher morality, which the ancient Greeks and Elizabethans turned into an art form. "We have art," writes Nietzsche, "in order not to die of truth."[14]

Even many humanitarians do not fully comprehend the tragic sensibility. They do not accept that their hard-nosed, realist adversaries are also motivated by truth: a different truth, that is also moral. The statesman first owes loyalty to the citizens of his territory, whose interests must usually take precedence over wider universal ones. The state comes before humanity, in other words, especially in democracies whose citizens decide who leads them. This is how the triumph of one good over another good causes suffering. It is what is irremediably wrong in the world, what the Greeks knew could not be fixed.

One can argue, of course, about individual decisions made in the midst of crises, in which national interests might very well correspond with humanitarian interests if only policymakers were wise enough to realize it. But the larger point still holds. National and humanitarian interests often clash, and even the wisest humanitarians can never be right all the time: therein lies tragedy.

To believe that the power of the United States can always right the world is a violation of the tragic sensibility. And yet significant elements of our foreign policy elite in Washington have subscribed to this notion. Because policy itself is a process that seeks to improve — ideally to fix — innumerable conditions abroad, the elite trusts that every problem is fixable, and that to disagree with this constitutes fatalism. But if that were true, tragedy would not exist. Tragedy is about bravely trying to fix the world, but only within limits, while knowing that many struggles are poignant and tragic precisely because they are futile. Since statesmanship is first and foremost about discipline and difficult choices, the greatest statesmen must think tragically. They think ahead with anxious foresight in order to avoid the worst outcomes. If, as Henry Kissinger once quipped, American elites are unique in their disdain for realism and realists, it can only be because they have no sense of the tragic: no awareness that struggle is not only about seeking justice but about seeking the lesser evil in an intractable world. There are many ways to fail, and some are better than others.

Abraham Lincoln and Franklin Roosevelt had the tragic sensibility in abundance. Lincoln consciously wrought terrible suffering upon the civilians of the South in 1864 to accomplish the greater good of ending the Civil War decisively. Roosevelt sent military aid to the mass murderer Stalin in order to defeat the mass murderer Hitler. Tragedy is often about accepting the lesser evil. It is a mindset that was much less required when the United States was protected by two oceans, in the decades and centuries before Pearl Harbor. Even after Pearl Harbor, power was usually in the hands of war veterans, from Harry Truman to Dwight D. Eisenhower, to George H. W. Bush, whose idealism and determination to improve the world were helpfully tempered by youthful rite-of-passage experiences with violent conflict. The current policy elite, by contrast, comprises the most physically and financially secure generation in American history. They may have suffered as individuals, but not as a group to the extent of previous generations, which accounts for their trouble in thinking tragically. In the late summer of 2021, President Joe

Biden and his advisers did not think sufficiently tragically about the withdrawal of U. S. troops they had ordered from Afghanistan. They did not consider worst-case scenarios, and chaos ensued.

To accept tragedy means to know that things often go wrong, and often have unintended consequences. Young veterans of Afghanistan and Iraq know this better than much older policy types in Washington who have never worn a uniform or reported on a war. That is why the most emotionally sophisticated students I have encountered as a teacher have been at military war colleges. The European immigrant intellectuals to the United States in the early and mid-twentieth century – people like Robert Strausz-Hupé, Hans Morgenthau, Zbigniew Brzezinski, and Henry Kissinger – harbored this tragic sensibility owing to their own life experiences. As Morgenthau wrote, "To improve the world, one must work with" the basest forces of human nature, "not against them."[15] This is neither cynicism nor pessimism, which would have nothing to do with attempts to advance humanity, but a tragic sensibility which recognizes that because there is something irremediably wrong with the world, the hero requires all the cunning at his disposal. Machiavelli, of course, was among the first to bring this view into Western political thought.

Geopolitics – the battle of space and power played out over a geographical setting – is inherently tragic. Policymaking, which seeks to right the world, is not. But because the tragic sensibility is a fusion of fatalism *and* struggle, successful statesmanship requires both. To believe only in geopolitics is lowering and cynical, but to advance policy solutions with no regard to geopolitics is arrogant and naive – the map, indeed, imposes limits. To think tragically means to see the world and international relations whole, in all of their aspects. "The fullness of life," Hamilton writes, "is in the hazards of life."[16]

All of us can make lists of writers, beyond the Greeks and Shakespeare, who majestically embody the tragic sensibility in all or some of its aspects: Fyodor Dostoevsky in *Demons,* Joseph Conrad in *Lord Jim,* George Eliot in *Daniel Deronda,* Alfred, Lord Tennyson in *Locksley Hall,* and Henry James in *The Princess Casamassima* are merely a few odd examples of my own. But perhaps the writing that most fully approaches the clarity of the ancient Greeks is not fiction or theater but a work of political philosophy: *The Federalist Papers,* by Alexander Hamilton, James Madison, and John Jay. Like the fifth-century BC Greeks and the sixteenth- and early seventeenth-century Elizabethans, the Founders of the American Republic in the late eighteenth century lived at a time of great possibilities and hope. Precisely because of their good fortune – mixed with the great personal risks they had taken in the Revolution – they could see all the dangers inherent in their new political experiment. It was only because they thought tragically about the human condition, and were themselves steeped in the Greek and Roman classics, that they allowed for a nation of optimists to follow in their wake.

Here is Hamilton in Federalist 6: "Men are ambitious, vindictive, and rapacious. To look for . . . harmony between a number of independent, unconnected sovereignties situated in the same neighborhood would be to disregard the uniform course of human events, and to set at defiance the accumulated experience of ages." And Madison in Federalist 10: "So strong is the propensity of mankind to fall into mutual animosities that where no substantial occasion presents itself the most frivolous and fanciful distinctions have been sufficient to kindle their unfriendly passions and excite their most violent conflicts." He goes on to say that "the *causes* of faction cannot be removed and . . . relief is only to be sought in the means of controlling its *effects.*"[17] *The Federalist Papers* famously continue like this.

10

They are an exercise in thinking tragically – relentlessly so – in order to prevent tragedy.

The Founders worried as much about chaos as they did about tyranny. In this sense as well, they adhered to the Greek tradition. "Few races have valued reason as much as the Greeks," writes F. L. Lucas. "But they [the Greeks] were too reasonable to ignore the power of the non-rational . . . For this non-rational side of the human spirit they created an immortal symbol – Dionysus." Dionysus was the "patron-god of Tragedy," the god with whom the writhing stage chorus was associated. He was the god of arousal, ecstasy, dreams, fantasies, fanaticisms, and ultimately of chaos.[18] Churchill, who had spent much of his life reading and writing history, and experiencing colonial wars firsthand as a soldier and war correspondent, had an intuition about Dionysus. Churchill had a rich historical imagination, having participated in one of the last horse-mounted cavalry charges in history in 1898 in Sudan, and had seen monsters as a young man. Thus, he saw through Hitler before almost anyone else in the British establishment.[19] The late Harvard classicist Charles Segal writes that tragedy exists as an art form so that "we may not forget the dimensions of life" that exist beyond the structures of civilization. Without "the painful possibility of seeing life as chaos," our civilized order "would become sterile, self-enclosed, solipsistic," and we ourselves would become arrogant with the hubris of our own intellectual power.[20] Tragedy depicts the struggle to wrest meaning and order out of savagery and anarchy. Carlyle depicted the French Revolution as the ultimate tragic drama of politics – one with no way out, it seems – since it was about "Anarchy against corrupt worn-out authority."[21]

Once again, within this vast panorama remains the individual, vast multitudes of them, often enough heroic. In Shakespeare's eyes, perhaps the supreme tragic hero of his time – someone who refused to compromise with the mediocrity of politics as it was then practiced, and so ended his life on the scaffold – was the Earl of Essex: a military leader both ambitious and charismatic, who nevertheless failed and did so tragically.[22]

The tragic sensibility says that there is nothing more beautiful in this world than the individual's struggle against long odds, even as death awaits him. Mortality, wrote the Spanish philosopher Miguel de Unamuno in 1912, lies at the root of the tragic sensibility. He quotes Flaubert as identifying a time in antiquity when people had stopped truly believing in the pagan gods but long before Christianity had fully emerged – the period between Cicero and Marcus Aurelius: "a unique moment in which man stood alone," with a short lifespan and nothing to look forward to beyond the grave. Never before or since, Flaubert writes, was there such "grandeur" in the human spirit.[23] The Greek poet C. P. Cavafy writes movingly about the example of the Greek heroes of Thermopylae facing certain death and defeat. *Grandeur,* now that is the very essence of tragedy.

The most commanding and densely brilliant interpretation of tragedy I am aware of is Maurice Bowra's *Sophoclean Tragedy,* first published in 1944. My own paperback reprint from 1965, faded and disintegrating, is protected by a clear plastic cover, as I am constantly taking it off the shelf to search for a quote, or an insight, the way others comb through Thucydides. Bowra fought at Ypres, Passchendaele, and Cambrai and "was buried alive when a trench collapsed," writes a biographer; he "saw and smelt death on a daily basis." He came out of World War I with a deep loathing of war and military strategists. Yet he always believed in duty and consequently hated pacifism, too. Having seen Hitler in the flesh at a mass rally while on a visit to Germany, from his perch at Oxford Bowra became a hater of appeasement.[24] Like Churchill, he had come face to face with demons, and this familiarity was vital to the quality of his thinking and writing.

Life experience, or the lack of it, continues to define generations of academics. I know that whatever value my own work might have, if it has any, is the consequence not only of books I have read but of places and circumstances I have experienced firsthand as a foreign correspondent: the tyrannical regimes of communist Eastern Europe during the Cold War, the chaos of Liberia and Sierra Leone in the 1990s, the tyranny and chaos of Syria and Iraq in the twentieth and twenty-first centuries, and so forth. Chaos especially is hard to communicate unless one has experienced its bowel-churning reality up close. There is nothing like the memory of naked physical insecurity to concentrate one's thinking — to know at the most vivid, tangible level what exactly is war, what is tyranny, and what is chaos. In my mind, Bowra's insights, as well as those of his contemporaries, are more valuable than those of many present-day academics who have never known physical and economic insecurity — and who have never known moral humiliation. My own moral humiliations are the knowledge that a book I wrote had the result, however unintended, of delaying a president's response to mass murder in the Balkans, and that I helped promote a war in Iraq that resulted in hundreds of thousands of deaths. These, taken together, have burdened my sleep for decades, wrecking me at times and motivating me to write this book. (The reader will judge if these misfortunes have given me some qualification to do so.)

Bowra, like Hegel and Edith Hamilton, knows that the greatest writers of tragedy were the Greeks and Shakespeare. And like all the scholars I have quoted, he knows that at the root of tragedy, both Greek and Elizabethan, lay "abrupt and unforeseen changes of fortune which engage profound interest and sympathy" and which, despite all the intervening "horror," ultimately "provide peace." But he also informs us of the chief difference between the Greeks and Shakespeare. Whereas the Greek tragic playwrights depict men before the gods, Shakespeare depicts good and evil men and women in conflict with each other. The Greeks are religious whereas Shakespeare is not. As Bowra writes, "In every play of Sophocles, the gods take an active, even a decisive, part. Their will is done, even though men resist it." But in Shakespeare, despite supernatural moments such as the appearance of witches in *Macbeth* and the Ghost in *Hamlet,* the evil that utterly wrecks characters like Lear and Othello "is not in their stars" but in their own deficiencies of character. In Sophocles (perhaps more so in Aeschylus, less so in Euripides) men are archetypes, and so are essentially of the same rough mold.[25] Yet in Shakespeare, it isn't only Hamlet who is lavishly realized as an individual whose misfortunes must inevitably be self-inflicted. So too are Iago, Lear, Macbeth, Cleopatra, and everyone else who inhabits his plays. Is there any character in literature more tactile and singular than Iago? The devil-in-the-flesh, he is brave, daring, and shameless; a veritable genius of style and manipulation, who exists only to scheme and destroy others. Is there anyone as good and altogether wholesome on this earth as Lear's daughter Cordelia; or as passionate as Cleopatra? For Shakespeare, character is fate. For the Greeks, the gods are.

Taken together, the Greeks and Shakespeare encompass all that is archetypal and all that is human, all that is good and all that is evil. Here is life in the full, and nothing brings it out into the open — nothing dissects the machine of fortune in such terrifying and absolute simplicity—as the tragic mind at work. It both endures and abides suffering so that order can ultimately triumph over chaos and the world can find some degree of solace.

To abide suffering is a hard, unpleasant truth with which the tragic sensibility can nevertheless live. It cannot, as I said, live with unspeakable crimes that exist beyond the pale of tragedy. The tragic mind is deeply humane, even as it is deeply realistic. As Hegel understood, tragedy appeals to the spirit because it is itself about a conflict of the spirit. Statues of the gods are sublime only when they are alone and in repose, not when they are in conflict with each other.[26] The Greek achievement was to show us that this is not a contradiction.

In this book I argue for thinking tragically in order to avoid tragedy. Doing so requires a journey into the Greek and Shakespearean canons, and also into the parts of the modern Western canon most relevant to the difficult truths identified by the ancients and the Elizabethans. For example, there are the nineteenth-century Germans, who focused obsessively on philosophy in order not to compete with the protean genius of Goethe, which dominated all the other literary genres in Germany for so long.

I will not be a conventional guide for this journey. My knowledge comes from decades of intense experience observing war, anarchy, and oppression at close range in Eurasia and Africa, from Iraq to Romania to Sierra Leone—as well as from my professional misfortunes and mistakes. It was an urge to make sense of what I had seen and experienced that led me to explore the great works of history and literature. In the guise of fiction, a writer can more easily tell the truth, letting make-believe characters express his or her actual beliefs. This is why no political science methodology can match the insights of the Greeks, Shakespeare, and the great novelists. And their most powerful and deepest insights are all situated within the crucible of tragedy, which holds the key to understanding a world in upheaval, where the struggle against Dionysian chaos is unrelenting.

Chapter 2

THE AGE OF DIONYSUS

The workings of nature are at once "unforeseeable and ineluctable," wrote the late British literary critic Tony Tanner. He was describing the downfall and destruction of Coriolanus, that brutal force of muscular action and agency who, nevertheless, is crushed by a machine called fate in Shakespeare's last great tragedy.[1] Tragedy is the comprehension that the human order is confounded by such mysteries, and so the tragic mind deals with the contradictions of humanity's place in nature.[2] And humanity's place in nature, the fact that we can exist only within nature – not exclusively in some exalted world of technology and rational choice – is demonstrated by the fact that our behavior and decision-making are influenced by emotional drives and physical instincts that we ourselves barely control, whatever our pretensions.

This is why Dostoevsky and Conrad have such a disturbing effect upon readers. In Dostoevsky's *Crime and Punishment*, not just Raskolnikov but many of the characters are disheveled, impulsively self-destructive, and given to illusions and ecstasies, yet you never doubt the truth of their existence. Conrad's *Under Western Eyes*, set in the deranged world of Russian anarchists in Geneva on the eve of the Russian Revolution, depicts nothing less than human beasts in the jungle. Dostoevsky and Conrad — both Slavs, from beyond the confines of Western Europe — comprehend the world the way the Greeks, with their own Eastern influences, did: they know that if the irrational is not given its proper place, the human world — and what is likely to happen in it — simply cannot be understood.[3]

The Greek playwrights paid homage to the mysterious, to the incomprehensible, and to the irrational. The ancient chorus itself was "the symbol of the whole mass in Dionysian arousal," in Nietzsche's words, explicitly celebrating Dionysus, the god of chaos and ecstasy, in dramatic festivals held in his honor.[4] This does not mean that the Greeks championed chaos; only that they accepted it as a reality that always lay just over the horizon. For the Greeks, the world was beautiful precisely because they could be so realistic about it. And it is a mark of serious literature in any era that chaos thus is acknowledged.

Witness Shakespeare. The Norwegian crown prince Fortinbras, surveying the heap of bodies at the end of *Hamlet*, notes the "havoc" that the royal court of Denmark has wrought on itself. Hamlet's faithful friend Horatio, seeing the same pitiable sight, observes:

> . . . . So shall you hear
> Of carnal, bloody, and unnatural acts,
> Of accidental judgments, casual slaughters,
> Of deaths put on by cunning and (forced) cause,
> And, in this upshot, purposes mistook
> Fall'n on th' inventors' heads.[5]

The play ends with Fortinbras moving to restore order, at the cost of a Norwegian takeover of Denmark. Yet order is paramount. It is the

—

first step toward civilization. Only afterward can the work begin to make order less coercive.

Yet to arrive at civilization requires never forgetting the world before and beyond civilization. This is where Shakespeare, even in the bad, early play *Titus Andronicus,* allows us to know our own archaic past—a time when bravery and courage are interchangeable with brutality and barbarism; a time when even a declaration of *honor* is a prelude to "some cruel and ruthless deed."[6] In this way literature becomes a substitute for collective memory. After a progression to writing about more refined eras in Roman history, Shakespeare returns, with *Coriolanus* near the close of his career, to this pre-civilized period of maniacal barbarity, when human beings were more archetypal, as if to bookend his oeuvre with the warning that we can never fully escape our origins. Modernity and now postmodernity have not altered human nature as much as we think. Hitler and Stalin were creatures of industrial modernism; Twitter and Facebook mobs and Internet conspiracy theories inflame the ethnic and religious hatreds of postindustrial postmodernism. The twenty-first century is still young, yet has seen monstrous, World War II–style military aggression by a nuclear-armed great power.

While civilization is the culmination of our struggle to realize our humanity and to rid ourselves of our propensity for violence and the iron grip of fate, we can only achieve this by never losing sight of our origins. But that is only possible by deliberately cultivating insecurity, whose broad basis is a respect for chaos: something impossible unless one thinks tragically.[7]

The cultivation of insecurity requires modesty. If a person—or a policymaker—is not modest, the gods will sooner or later force modesty upon them. And if a man has to wait until personal enlightenment is forced upon him by the gods, it will come with extreme suffering. We all eventually become humble, either in advance of personal catastrophe by always fearing for the future; or afterward, when the torment is that much greater. But no matter how wary we are regarding what-comes-next, the pandemonium of life with its numberless human interactions insures that at some point we will be crushed by something or other. This is why arrogance is a form of idiocy.

Nietzsche's brilliance lay in intuiting these things while still a young man. He published *The Birth of Tragedy* in 1872, when he was only twenty-eight, and its inspired, descriptive flights betray a youthful exuberance. The Greek world for him is defined by the contest between the rational "Apollonian art of the sculptor," with its deliberate and articulated form, and "the imageless Dionysian art of music," which is formless. Yet the lure of Dionysus is irresistible. His chariot, Nietzsche writes, "overflows with flowers and wreaths: beneath its yoke tread the panther and the tiger. If one were to allow one's imagination free rein in transforming Beethoven's 'Hymn to Joy' into a painting, particularly the moment when the multitudes kneel down awestruck in the dust, then one might come close to an idea of the Dionysian." To deny the power of Dionysian chaos, rapture, and intoxication is to deny the power of the creator himself.[8]

Dionysus does not signify doom so much as a world filled with rapturous mystery; so that the advent of a more rational and pessimistic worldview, as represented by Euripides, ironically indicates to Nietzsche the beginning of the end of tragedy.

Whereas Aeschylus and Sophocles wrote during the height of Athenian power, Euripides wrote later, at the time of the Peloponnesian War, which tore the Greek world apart in the last decades of the fifth century BC. He uses war as a means to look inward and examine the *polis*. War to him is a violent teacher.[9] Euripides' plays are infused with pessimism about political and military leadership and about human behavior in general. He despairs over the fact that reason will probably not outlast passion and persuasion will probably not outlast violence. No one would ever describe the disruptive, wondrous power of Dionysus as vividly as Euripides. Aristotle considered him the most deeply tragic of the Greek playwrights because of his emphasis on compassion and the fear of chaos, even while tragedy as a philosophical concept may have begun to die with him. Euripides' appeal is almost modern, because of his "fascination with argument, ideas and rhetoric" that reveal a universal and abstract sensibility. Yet this only leads to a profound pessimism about the human ability to control the forces of anarchy.[10] But tragedy was never meant to be that dark. In pure tragedy, struggle always has a purpose, a chance.

Nevertheless, Euripides, the indignant humanist who will not countenance human suffering, will not let humanity off the hook.[11] Though he recognizes fate, he will never accept it. As Hecuba retorts to Helen in *The Trojan Women*,

> Ah do not gloze
> Your fault by casting follies on the Gods,
> Lest fools alone should heed you![12]

Only the weak and the dishonest blame fate for their misfortunes, even as fate always affects our lives and may even periodically determine it. That is our dilemma: to accept moral responsibility though something may be only partly our fault (or not our fault at all). This is true of policy and politics as much as it is of private life. For much of the 1980s I reported firsthand on the Balkans, warning in print of impending ethnic and religious warfare there. But when such a war actually came in the early 1990s and the Clinton administration did not act in a timely fashion to save lives, my own writing was blamed for it, since my book *Balkan Ghosts* reportedly so depressed the president that it led to inaction on his part. While I supported military intervention in print and on television, my book had the opposite effect of what I intended. This led not so much to guilt on my part, as my motives had been good, but to lifelong remorse. Whatever my intentions, however much I had had the Balkans virtually to myself as a reporter in the 1980s before the media horde arrived, I had no choice but to accept moral responsibility.

Dionysus represents the most terrifying aspect of fate. He embodies the life force itself: that combustible element of the natural world in all its fecundity that makes civilization so tenuous a proposition because of humankind's basest physiological instincts, affecting personality and behavior. Dionysus is a complex figure, encompassing joy and celebration, violence and madness.[13] He is in effect the enemy of wisdom and reason. But while he must be resisted, the fanatical forces he unleashes can never be denied. The god's victory in this struggle is among the central stories of Greek tragedy.[14]

Euripides is horrified by Dionysian fanaticism. But he respects the vitality of its power and the unquestioning faith and ecstasy it generates. He wrote *The Bacchae* in old age and in voluntary exile in the exotic wilds of Macedonia, where the women still worshipped Dionysus. Here Euripides, the "lifelong rationalist," acknowledges the "terrible power of the irrational."[15]

In Greek mythology, the Bacchae (Bacchantes or Maenads, as they were also known) were women frenzied from wine. They rushed through the woods, swept up in ecstasy, emitting ferocious cries. "They would tear to pieces the wild creatures they met," Edith Hamilton writes, "and devour the bloody shreds of flesh." Nothing could restrain them. They translated beauty into fear, and joy into brutality. Their sources appear to be Asiatic: they migrated to Greece from the Near Eastern lands of Macedonia, Lydia, Phrygia, Persia, and Araby. In Robert Graves's rendering, Dionysus traveled as far as India and returned by way of Phrygia before heading for Thrace and Boetia, where "he invited the women to join his revels on Mount Cithaeron."[16] Euripides' *Bacchae* opens with these lines:

> Through the sun-scorched Persian uplands I have passed,
> Through Bactria's cities and the Medes' bleak marches,
> Through Araby the Blest and Asia's coasts . . .
> For Thebes must learn . . . My holy mysteries that she
> disdains . . .[17]

The mob in all its rage and terror—the Cossack pogrom, the Nazi mass rallies, the Serbian rape camps, the sectarian death squads—all contain elements of the fanaticism, the vitality, and the sheer deadly enthusiasm of the Bacchae. Nobel laureate Elias Canetti's insights into the phenomenon of crowd formation in *Crowds and Power* (1960) have a spiritual ancestor in Euripides' play, as Canetti defines the *crowd* as a mass of people who abandon their individuality in favor of an intoxicating collective symbol. In this, the impulse to destroy ultimately comes from the impulse to escape into an altered consciousness. The desire for ecstasy is inseparable from the desire for sleep. As Euripides writes,

> The liquid of the grape; that medicines
> Our sad humanity for all its sorrows,
> When the juice of the vine has filled them, bringing sleep
> And deep oblivion of daily cares.
> Toil knows no other balm . . .[18]

The Bacchae begins with Dionysus, disguised as a stranger, coming to Thebes to avenge himself against the house of Cadmus for denying his divinity. Cadmus and Tiresias, the blind seer, are wise enough not to make light of the god. But King Pentheus, Cadmus's grandson, is angry about the Maenads dancing crazily in the woods, especially since one of them is his own mother, Agave. Pentheus is determined, despite warnings from Cadmus and Tiresias, to stop the spread of Dionysus's new and terrifying cult. Pentheus's men capture and chain the still disguised Dionysus. Meanwhile, the Maenads have become more crazed and violent, literally ripping apart the flesh of a herd of cattle – the ultimate example of a senseless deed. Pentheus now vows to destroy the Maenads. But the disguised Dionysus casts a spell on Pentheus so that he dresses up as a woman and is ripped apart by the Maenads, including by Agave, still in her Dionysian trance.

> But foam flowed from her [Agave's] lips, wild rolled her eyes,
> And Dionysus held her soul possessed;
> Blind and infatuate, she heeded not,
> But seizing his [Pentheus's] left arm, and bearing hard
> With her foot against his flank, she wrenched away
> His shoulder . . .[19]

A delirious Agave returns in triumph to Thebes bearing the head of what she believes to be a lion she has killed, but which is in reality the head of her son and Cadmus's grandson, Pentheus. Cadmus shocks her out of her trance and in an instant she realizes the dreadful deed she has done. Dionysus then reveals himself in all his glory, the chorus singing his praise.

As Cadmus admits toward the end of the play,

———

Ah Dionysus has destroyed us—justly,
And yet too cruelly . . .[20]

This victory of chaos over established order shows how realism requires an appreciation for romance: stripped down to its essentials, romance is about ecstasy and irrationality; things that are part of reality. Thus to be unrelentingly rational is to be unrealistic. Wine, Euripides implies, is as necessary as dry thought.[21] And that, in turn, suggests that crises, especially political ones, deal not only with the clarity of decision-makers but also with their illusions. (Witness the neoconservative view that democracy could be imposed upon the Middle East.) Pentheus's ultimate crime is his all-knowing vanity. Again, because fate gets you in the end, struggle requires a respect for fate and therefore for a higher deity. What men deem sure, the gods bring to naught, says the Greek chorus at the end of *The Bacchae*.[22]

That specifically suggests a lesson for our own time. The very regularity of middle-class life promotes the illusion that the world is predictable and benign—a "complacency" that is "itself a kind of madness," writes the Indian novelist and environmentalist Amitav Ghosh. The planet, he continues, "has been toying with humanity," allowing it to assume a questionable freedom to shape its own destiny.[23] But human beings are now living by their hundreds of millions in dense urban concentrations along tropical seaboards in environmentally fragile terrain, subject to cyclones, super-storms, and sea level rises, in places that cannot sustain such numbers indefinitely. Super-storms and other catastrophes are the climatic equivalents of Dionysus. While so far it has mainly been those at the margins of economic existence, in places like Indonesia and

---

25

Bangladesh, who have suffered the earth's Dionysian wrath, we elites in our luxurious urban cocoons, made possible by delicate, critical infrastructure, should think tragically in order to prepare for a visit by the god. The pandemic of Covid-19 was but a wake-up call. Any other attitude would constitute hubris.

Besides environmental disorder there is social disorder. Henry James, that outwardly effete and Europeanized genius, actually shows us in a masterwork of detail, *The Princess Casamassima,* the underworld that polite society does not see, and which he discovered in his frequent nighttime walks through London: "peopled with a thousand forms of revolutionary passion and devotion. . . . In silence, in darkness, but under the feet of each one of us, the revolution lives and works. It is a wonderful, immeasurable trap, on the lid of which society performs its antics." Beware, James says, "the sophistries of civilization."[24]

Polite society has not changed and never will. It is a function of social success that one avoids discussing or even thinking about the cruelest facts of human nature and, by consequence, political existence. True, among the elite there is much virtue-signaling about the poor, and a vocal concern for human rights is a necessary tool of professional advancement in the high social echelons. A bored elite can certainly develop a brainless infatuation with radical causes. But that is not what I am talking about. I am talking about the silences inside which the future lies: the disturbing rumblings by which the working poor periodically prepare to throw bricks through the windows of the elite world, and to which the elite are blind until they are hit in the face. That is the ultimate meaning of Donald Trump's election victory in 2016. This is another form of Dionysian wrath: something which James, pampered as he was by wealth and social status, nevertheless had the wisdom and shrewd perception to be aware of.

It isn't only nature and society that are awash with Dionysian chaos. So too is the human mind—ultimately a creation of natural, biological processes. No writer intuits this better than Fyodor Dostoevsky. From the first pages of *Crime and Punishment* (1866), the full-bodied chaos and skin-of-one's-teeth struggle for survival is depicted as the heart of emotional existence. Life is torment. The novel's protagonist is an unceasing fount of maniacally racing thoughts. Whereas the Greeks make archetypes out of the human predicament and Shakespeare invented conscience itself, the first moderns—Dostoevsky, Henry James—replicate consciousness, showing the mind as it actually works. From the Greeks to Shakespeare to the moderns it is an increasingly inward journey, and the greatness of every writer in the canon is related to their ability to acknowledge the god Dionysus and all that he represents: above all, the impulse toward disintegration. That is finally why, as Dostoevsky explains in *Demons*, "the Greeks deified nature."[25] Thus we are back to Dostoevsky and Conrad and their closeness to the spirit of the Greeks: they both, to borrow from George Steiner, make a virtue of disorder, with calm achieved only through despair.[26] Anyone who has suffered a sustained, anxiety-ridden mental collapse of any sort understands this.

And anyone looking at the current international environment cannot but comply with the Greeks' fear of chaos, and admit to the attendant human proclivity for destructiveness. A third of a century after the fall of the Berlin Wall, which our elites, often with little real-life experience of their own, assured us would lead to the march of democracy and globalization, the world is in extreme disorder. Several major Middle Eastern countries have collapsed into chaos. The great powers — the United States, China, and Russia — edge closer to outright war as they build up vast arsenals of precision-guided weapons to accompany their navies and air forces, even as social media inflames ethnic, national, and religious divides. Simply because we can no longer literally imagine unrestrained war between the great powers — as the last one ended over three-quarters of a century ago — does not mean that it cannot happen, as it has happened throughout history. Just look at Ukraine! All this is to say nothing of the armed rebellions taking place in swaths of Africa and elsewhere that go underreported or ignored. No one can deny the Greeks their fears.

Chapter 3

ORDER: THE ULTIMATE NECESSITY

Among the chief attributes of Greek tragedy is its concision.
Each play is jammed with insights. Nietzsche considered tragedy
the greatest of Greek achievements. Its origins, explained best by the
British classicist Richard Seaford, lie in "a synthesis of two opposite
principles, the Dionysiac and the Apolline." The first, in the spirit of
the god Dionysus, is the realm of intoxication and rapturous unity
among people and with nature; the second, in the spirit of Apollo, is
the realm of limits, form, and structure.[1] The first principle is emotional and emphasizes the tyranny of the group; the second is analytical and emphasizes disciplined, individual thought. The Dionysian
spirit, while linked with a chaotic tyranny, also represents the life force
itself, which can be both positive and romantic. By contrast, the
Apolline spirit leads inexorably to disturbing thoughts, as Apollo, the
most Greek of all the gods, is both the bearer of logic and the god of
truth. Because passion is the enemy of analysis and vice versa, it follows that Dionysus and Apollo are in opposition. Nietzsche also saw
in Greek tragedy a balance between optimism and pessimism.[2]
Because of this tension, tragedy is the very embodiment of rigorous

thinking. This balance often contradicts the etiquette of our policy elites, at whose gatherings for many years it helped to declare oneself an "optimist," especially about the prospects of democracy in this or that Middle Eastern country, regardless of one's actual instincts on the issue at hand, since being an "optimist" improves one's moral standing within the group. But however salonfahig, this behavior is neither systematic nor rational. Tragedy rises above virtue-signaling.

Tragedy also rises above the blithe assumption that the end of the Cold War would lead to the unimpeded spread of democracy and free markets worldwide; to the assumption held by virtually the entire East Coast policy elite that the more we traded with China and the richer China became, the more liberal China's government and society would become; and to the assumption, also once widely held by the elite, that the spread of NATO throughout Central and Eastern Europe would lead to universally liberal societies, including Russia's, and that economic shock therapy would deliver a democratic and wholesome capitalist society in Russia itself. All those positions were once shared by significant elements of the Washington and New York policy nomenklatura, with few dissenters. And all disregarded the Dionysian element in tragedy. For a short while even, in the early Clinton administration, there were people who believed that with the Cold War ended, geopolitics had disappeared from history and had been replaced by geoeconomics. Of course what would actually occur was the merging of geopolitics with geoeconomics to form an even more dangerous and volatile witches' brew. Yes, Dionysus would have his revenge as ethnic and religious warfare shook the Balkans, the Middle East, and Africa; and as a new form of cold war erupted between the United States and China, and between the United States and Russia. Russia could indeed emerge as a democracy after Vladimir Putin's downfall. But if that happens, it will do so in an internally driven, messy, organic process, not by imposition from outside.

Because Apollo and Dionysus coexist and intertwine, the tension between civilization and savagery is constant and ubiquitous. Savagery is not confined to the margins of civilization but exists right in the heart of the polis.[3] As Freud wrote, "Civilized society is perpetually menaced with disintegration."[4] Even the most exalted and refined societies are in constant danger of internal upheaval and breakdown. Social decadence can lead to barbarism; but so can invasion, domestic unrest, and normal, insidious political evolution. Barbarism always lies within us. And one year of anarchy can be worse than many more years of tyranny, as I can attest from long visits to Iraq both before and after Saddam Hussein was toppled.[5] Of course, order itself can be oppressive and tyrannical; and thus constant evolutions away from tyranny are to be encouraged. Yet a simple-minded opposition to tyranny conveniently avoids the core question: What if there were no order at all? In Iraq I was besieged by artillery from several directions, fired not by a rival army but by a throng of small militia groups. In Sierra Leone I was threatened by drunken soldiers wearing only parts of uniforms at makeshift roadblocks in the forest. Even the worst regime is less dangerous and terrifying than no regime at all. Because policy elites are in love with ideas, they fear tyranny that can suppress their ideas. But because they have never had to negotiate roadblocks in Africa run by men demanding bribes with the safeties on their assault rifles switched off, they lack a visceral fear of anarchy.

The Russian masses in 1917 also lacked a visceral fear of anarchy and where it might lead. They believed their revolution had ended in triumph with the abdication of Czar Nicholas II, not realizing that, as medieval and tyrannical as the Romanovs were, they represented the only order to be had in Russia. With their overthrow came a complete breakdown of institutions that led, in turn, to a Bolshevik coup later in the year that would have the effect of murdering and enslaving tens of millions for decades on end.

Indeed, order comes before freedom, since without order there can be no freedom or liberty for anybody. Baby boomers and later generations in the United States have difficulty with this concept because they are the first generations in human history to have grown up with both physical and financial security. Their lack of experience makes them blind to what existence without such security truly feels like. Taking order completely for granted, they are concerned only with making it less oppressive. In other words, our current generations have not been conditioned to think tragically.

But all previous generations in human history have been obsessed by order. Without it there is no one to adjudicate right from wrong, to separate the guilty from the innocent, so not only is there no freedom but also, as Hobbes famously wrote, no justice. This is why Shakespeare considered monarchy the most natural form of government. Even today, the most stable and civil regimes in the Arab world are traditional monarchies, given that most attempts at democracy have failed and secular dictatorships have compensated for their lack of historical legitimacy with extreme forms of brutality. Witness the Baathist regimes in Syria and Iraq, and the Gaddafi regime in Libya.

Monarchy works because, at the end of the day, tradition is everything. As Albert Camus explains, tradition provides "eternal answers and commentaries," which are sacred.[6] We have nothing else. What is ceremony, after all? The investitures of British kings and queens, the inauguration of American presidents, with all the marching bands? It is "the panoply and mystique of power and hierarchy" that reinforces order, writes the late British critic Tony Tanner. Authority requires awe, from which emerges legitimacy. The tribunes who murder Shakespeare's Julius Caesar because he has become a dictator do away with his "ceremonious" aspect and reduce him, in Tanner's words, to "the poor, forked, fallible, physical body he undoubtedly is." Yet in killing Caesar, those driving for freedom only pave the way to anarchy, with more brutal murders to come, until another Roman dictator rises to restore order, and with it, ceremony.[7]

We live in an age in which ceremony has been debased, and not only by the Kardashian-like glitz and decadence of the Trump presidency. It is an age of crumbling hierarchies and weakening institutions: in government, work, religion, and social and sexual relations. Of course, hierarchies can be unfair and oppressive. But dismantling them brings the responsibility to erect new and fairer hierarchies, since the question of order remains paramount. In many Greek tragedies, the plot is the destruction of order through some act, which leads to madness and disorder, until order is restored. Because this has been the pattern throughout human history, why should it not continue?

The first Greek who took up this problem in literature was Aeschylus. Aeschylus wrote the *Oresteia* trilogy when he was nearly seventy, in the mid-fifth century BC. The late classicist F. L. Lucas calls Aeschylus "the stern old soldier of Marathon; the somewhat aloof aristocrat . . . hating alike tyranny and anarchy, the type of Athenian as yet untouched by decadence."[8] His *Oresteia* trilogy dramatizes the contrast "between a darker world of vendetta and savage intrafamilial conflict and a society in which the rule of law has an important place," writes another classicist, Richard Rutherford.[9]

Though Aeschylus is in spirit a democrat because he acknowledges the constant threat of anarchy, he is above all an analyst. And analysis is central to Greek tragedy: the depiction of passion from a viewpoint of dispassion. It is a similar sense of dispassion and distance that underlies the particular dramatic effect in the paintings of Velázquez.

The background to the *Oresteia* trilogy begins with Thyestes, the son of Pelops, who has seduced the wife of his brother, Atreus. As revenge, Atreus kills two of Thyestes' sons, cooks their flesh, and serves them to the unknowing Thyestes for dinner. When Thyestes learns what he has eaten he curses the race of Atreus forever. The curse is visited upon Atreus's son, King Agamemnon. Agamemnon seals his doom when he decides to sacrifice his daughter Iphigenia to the goddess Artemis, so that the goddess will send favorable winds for the invasion force he is leading against Troy. In her rage at what her husband has done, Agamemnon's wife, Queen Clytemnestra, takes for a lover Aegisthus, another of Thyestes' sons, and together they murder Agamemnon with an axe in his bath soon after his triumphant return to Mycenae from Troy. Thus ends *Agamemnon*, the first play of the trilogy.

The *Choephoroe* ("The Libation-Bearers"), the trilogy's second play, is named for Clytemnestra's women servants, whom the queen, in a fit of guilt, sends to offer propitiatory libations for her dead husband. Years later, Orestes, the son of Agamemnon and Clytemnestra, returns to Mycenae from abroad to pray at his father's tomb. Here he meets his sister, Electra, and together they swear vengeance against their mother and her lover, both of whom Orestes subsequently slays. Now, in the second generation, it is Orestes, rather than Clytemnestra, who is stained with blood defiled by an evil deed: matricide, an aberration of the laws of nature that will unleash the

Furies against him. Orestes flees in exile to northern Greece, where he becomes the founder of Kastoria, a place of often leaden skies, the crunch of dead poplar leaves, and mountains grooved with snow.

In the *Eumenides* ("The Kind Goddesses"), the last play of the trilogy, Orestes travels from Kastoria to Apollo's shrine at Delphi to hide from the Furies — crones with snakes for hair who torment the young for crimes committed against their elders. At Delphi, the Oracle commands Orestes to go to Athens to stand trial for his mother's murder. There he is acquitted after admitting his sin, and the Furies are persuaded to remain in Athens and reign as "the kind goddesses." Justice prevails, and the cycle of violence is finally ended. Passion leads to disorder, before order eventually triumphs. But it is only the fear of a secular authority that helps undergird such justice. This is a familiar story, but the *Oresteia* trilogy is the first great epic to tell it.

Of course, the *Oresteia*'s plot and its interpretations are far more complex than I have made them. Read the second volume of Robert Graves's *The Greek Myths* (1955 and 1960) for the full majesty and granularity of it. Moreover, bear in mind the vivid, spectacular effect of these plays when first performed on stage to an audience 2,500 years ago: the children of Agamemnon beating on his grave; "the wild incantations of the Chorus rousing the murdered monarch in his sepulcher"; the honey-haired Apollo facing the Gorgon-like Furies; "the torchlight procession at the close."[10]

Shakespeare, too, is obsessed with order. Witness his first play, *Titus Andronicus,* an archaic "parody" set in ancient Rome that, to listen to the late Harold Bloom, seems in a sense more "remote" than the *Oresteia.*[11] Yet *Titus Andronicus* has its value. As in the *Oresteia,* precisely because of human passions and blunders, order quickly descends into a grand guignol of violence, "a wilderness of tigers," with murders, executions, and amputations as one character after another is butchered before peace and order are finally restored.[12]

Am I belaboring the obvious? Not if the overwhelming tendency of modern literature is to ignore this entire question and deal instead with issues of love and sexual relations, professional and class tensions, and all manner of personal and psychological dramas. That is because order, like the air we breathe, is so completely taken for granted – since in our middle-class world and the world of fellow elites elsewhere, relatively few have experienced any form of existence beyond their predictable, regulated lives, which became even more regulated for a time because of a pandemic. Except for war veterans, foreign correspondents, migrants, and immigrants, disorder is something most people know only through the imagination. But order remains the fundamental question behind the politics of many countries, even big states like Russia, China, and Brazil. Even we in the United States may not be as secure as we believe. Our democratic order was a philosophical and institutional inheritance from early modern England, and it took England 700 years to ascend from the Magna Carta to women's suffrage, with many violent dynastic struggles in between. The traditions of democracy, as our follies in the Arab world demonstrate, are not built overnight. The foundations on which we stand took centuries to construct and may still be more fragile than we believe, a fact evinced by the hyperpartisanship of both our media and political parties. Literature that recognizes this insecurity is of the most profound kind.

And so we are back to Joseph Conrad in *Under Western Eyes*. In the author's note to that book, Conrad suggests that human communities have often oscillated tragically between the "ferocity and imbecility of an autocratic rule" and "the no less imbecile and atrocious answer" of utopian ideals.[13] Achieving a balance between those extremes has been a painfully constructed political work of art.

Goethe "loathed disorder," George Steiner notes; he "preferred injustice" since "injustice is temporary and reparable whereas disorder destroys the very possibilities of human progress." Of course, as Steiner also notes, "it is the individual instance of injustice that infirms the general pretense of order." After all, just "one Hamlet is enough to convict a state of rottenness."[14] This accounts for the outrage of intellectuals and journalists railing against the imperfections of even the most democratic states. And it is this outrage that guards democracies from slipping into repression at home despite the compromises they must make in their relations abroad, for which these same intellectuals have little sympathy. The problem is, as that wily observer of the human condition Anthony Trollope realizes in *Phineas Finn*, to "inveigh against existing evils," while being yourself free of bureaucratic responsibilities, is a very convenient situation to be in.[15] It puts you always on the side of the right while requiring no difficult choices, so that you may treat morality as an inflexible absolute.

Albert Camus was an exception. He valued order. In one of his greatest books, *The Rebel*, he writes that "an act of rebellion . . . seems like a demand for clarity and unity. The most elementary form of rebellion, paradoxically, expresses an aspiration to order." Furthermore, "When the throne of God is overturned, the rebel realizes that it is now his own responsibility to create the justice, order, and unity that he sought in vain within his own condition, and in this way to justify the fall of God."[16] By itself, the toppling of kings and tyrants does not always morally justify the rebel. Toppling a suffocating dictatorship in the Middle East is not by itself a moral act,

---

unless one has developed a plan for something better. The rebel must replace the old order with a new one that is more just, or at least more benign. Communism was in the end illegitimate because, once it declared the capitalist order dead, the new ideology was expected to advance its own moral universe, which it signally failed to do. Here Camus's philosophy is aligned with traditional statesmanship and in opposition to intellectuals whose celebration of revolt is often narcissistic and not linked to the restitution of order.

Tyrannies do not govern in a vacuum. They often do so from a base of at least some popular support. This is a truth more alien to the American experience than to Camus's. His nightmare is that rebellion can lead to even worse tyrannies than the ones we have. And yet, as he says, ever since Prometheus rebelled against Zeus in the deserts of Scythia, revolt has been a distinguishing characteristic of humanity. It has been built into the human condition ever since people first became slaves. The decayed and reptilian regimes toppled in Tunisia and Egypt at the beginning of the Arab Spring, characterized by obscene cults of personality with little promise of reform, robbed people of their dignity and consequently made them feel like slaves. Every giant poster of the leader told people that they were nothing. But while rebellion against tyranny is natural, erecting a new order is not. Order is nothing we should ever take for granted. Camus devotes a whole book to this realization.

To drive his point home, Camus, in a related essay, extolls Herman Melville's last great story, *Billy Budd*, as a commentary on the tragic necessity of order above all other concerns. As Camus explains, "In allowing the young sailor, a figure of beauty and innocence whom he dearly loves, to be condemned to death, Captain Vere submits his heart to the law. And at the same time, with this flawless story that can be ranked with certain Greek tragedies, the aging Melville tells us of his acceptance . . . of the sacrifice of beauty and innocence so that order may be maintained and the ship of men may continue to move forward toward an unknown horizon."[17]

Like *Moby-Dick*, *Billy Budd* is biblical, if only the Old and New Testaments were as densely analytical as Melville. Billy Budd is a childlike sailor with a stutter, who can't defend himself with his tongue when he is falsely accused of a serious crime and ends up, in his frustration, using his fists. The false accuser, Captain Vere exclaims, is thus "'struck dead by an angel of God. Yet the angel must hang!" Otherwise, mutiny would ensue. This is a culture – a British ship in the midst of fighting the Napoleonic Wars – far removed from civilian life and dependent for its survival on the maintenance of strict order. And so Captain Vere painfully, regretfully bows to necessity: Billy Budd's subsequent execution mirrors a crucifixion. "For us here," Vere explains, "acting not as casuists or moralists, it is a case practical, and under martial law practically to be dealt with."[18]

Melville, through the voice of Captain Vere, goes on: "Do these buttons that we wear attest that our allegiance is to Nature? No, to the King. . . . We fight at command . . . however pitiless that law may operate in any instances, we nevertheless adhere to it and administer it . . . let not warm hearts betray heads that should be cool."[19]

Melville's genius is that he also cries in his soul at the unjustness, yet in the end unambiguously justifies the execution. He knows that there is something irredeemably wrong with the world that cannot be fixed. This makes him among the most Greek of all the moderns.

Melville's attitude should not be confused with fatalism – throwing one's hands up and submitting to cruelty and heartlessness. Only those who do not wield bureaucratic power have the

---

luxury of such an accusation. Those in power have to act according to their oath. This is why the ideal tragedy, according to Camus, is about this "first and foremost tension." Remember that Zeus, who "pitilessly oppresses" Prometheus, "also has right on his side."[20]

The masses, the media especially, unsatisfied with such difficult realities, demand unambiguous moral resolution to such questions, but often there can be none.

Chapter 4

ORDER AND NECESSITY MUST BE OBEYED, EVEN WHEN THEY ARE UNJUST

When *The Birth of Tragedy* was published, the twenty-eight-year-old Nietzsche had already been a professor at the University of Basel for a few years. The book provoked controversy because it attacked the complacent rationalism of late nineteenth-century Germany by comparing it to the standards of Greek tragedy, with the latter's exalted fusion of Dionysian chaos and Apolline form. Young and a bit impetuous as he was, Nietzsche had already developed his trademark ability to disturb through uncomfortable truths — much as the Greeks disturb. He explains that Zeus was not altogether wrong in his endless torturing of Prometheus, the Titan whose indomitable spirit engages our sympathy. Prometheus represented a challenge, however noble, to Zeus's rule, and Zeus was well within his rights (as he interpreted them) to keep an eagle tearing away at chained Prometheus's liver. It is such unnerving insights, Nietzsche tells us, that make the Greeks great.[1]

True tragedy is "godlike" and thus unsatisfying, according to Hegel, since it always presents both sides of an argument as "justified." Each side is bound by "necessity" to seek its ends. The fact is, many of our actions are "yoked beneath Necessity," as Aeschylus writes in *Agamemnon*. "It is the stars," says Kent in *King Lear*, "The stars above us govern our conditions." We often do what we must, or how we think we must. It is the postmodern delusion that we are free to choose and decide on everything we do. But there are always a million constraints upon us. Only the independently wealthy have some of the freedom that, according to the self-help industry, so many of us have.

Bound by necessity, we are forced into struggle with one another. Justice only exists in opposing the "one-sidedness" in each of our claims, and thus in seeing things from both points of view. Tragedy can be like the ultimate trial case, the reason that the Supreme Court, when it is not degraded by partisanship, can offer up the most rarified arguments to decide the fate of men and women whose claims are irreconcilable. "The reason why the tragic conflict appeals to the spirit is it is itself a conflict of the spirit," Hegel writes. Whereas we imagine the gods as depicted in Greek statuary in solitary peace, tragedy shows that they are in constant collision. While "their nature is divine," they often "meet as foes."[2] The gods, as mirrors of human nature, are impelled into conflict with each other.

Whatever the gods do, however unjust they may be, they must be honored. Maurice Bowra writes that it is a modern conceit that the gods treat Oedipus unfairly — deciding on his terrible fate before he is even born and then inflicting it on him without mercy. "This is not a view that Sophocles would have held," Bowra dryly observes. Sophocles believed that humans cannot judge the gods and, as Heraclitus said, for the gods "all things are beautiful and just."[3] Thus when we defy the gods, we are punished.

This is fatalism on one level, but on a higher level it guards against pride and inculcates the awareness that there are always

---

42

things about the world and about situations that we cannot know, and which therefore should make us humble. The mysteries of the gods that we cannot know are metaphorical signatures of facts on the ground in distant countries and places that Washington policymakers, for example, cannot be aware of, and which upend their plans. It isn't just Iraq and Afghanistan that have humbled policymakers. So have places like Nigeria, South Africa, and Ethiopia, which for years were said to be making progress and were therefore good investment opportunities, yet which descended into civil conflict, war, and failed-state status at one level or another. Like Oedipus, we become wise only in our awareness of our own incomplete knowledge. It is our very powerlessness to know and dominate everything that, Bowra suggests, "should bring [us] peace of mind." As for the exceptional among us, who rise to great positions of power, sooner or later they come into direct conflict with their fellows and with the gods. And the gods always win over those who are not, at the end of the day, humble in some crucial way. Tragedy is complete only when the protagonist comprehends his own insignificance. The Greeks are relentless in driving home this point. They "depict levels of suffering from which modern sensibility shrinks."[4]

To comprehend your own insignificance is neither defeatism nor cowardice but the opposite. Once again, to act, and to act bravely, even in the face of no great result, constitutes the ultimate in human grandeur, and brings us back to what tragedy is about. Schopenhauer boils it down brutally: "He who is without hope is also without fear."[5] He calls this desperation, but there can be a fine line between desperation and grandeur. Churchill evinced both at key moments in World War II. Remember that appeasement, when it happened in 1938 at Munich, was a superficially rational decision, since it promised to at least postpone a Europe-wide war after the previous one had killed many millions only twenty years earlier. Churchill was completely aware of this and of his own country's many weaknesses when the war began in earnest, yet he acted according to necessity, thoroughly without illusion. Appeasement had been an affront to his imperial pride. He knew the worldly equivalent of what Oedipus knew without having to be blinded, and was at peace with the awful weight of the world upon him. Churchill seemed to be aware that before the gods, he himself was insignificant. It was this inner peace, believing himself to be at the still point of a turning world, that gave him the ability to act. He thought tragically, which allowed him to avoid tragedy. Churchill was especially great between Munich and Pearl Harbor, when Great Britain stood alone up until America entered the war.

Tragedy is not fatalism; nor is it despair; nor is it related to the quietism of the Stoics. It is comprehension. By thinking tragically, one is made aware of all one's limitations, and thus can act with more effectiveness. Just as the gods struggle against each other, men and women struggle against the gods, so that fate and human agency are intertwined: fate often winning out when people do not think tragically enough. The *Iliad* is the greatest work on war because, by chronicling the machinations of gods and men, it attempts to explain why things happen as they do. Ultimately, according to Horace, only the gods can resolve the most difficult situations, but human agency is necessary to help this process. And because it is impossible to know at what precise juncture the gods must intervene, men and women must continue to struggle, even as they know there is a higher mechanism at work. That higher mechanism signifies nothing less than a form of order beyond that of men and women. It may be unjust, but like necessity, it must be accepted.

The two-decade-long American war in Afghanistan drama-tized the struggle between fate and human agency. President George W. Bush invaded Afghanistan only after the Taliban had failed to help apprehend the perpetrators of 9/11. The subsequent toppling of the Taliban regime was done with ingenuity and a minimum of military force. Our leaders appeared conscious of how the Afghans had humiliated the Soviets in the 1980s. It was only after the regime was toppled that the United States defense and security establish-ments stopped thinking tragically, by dispatching a big army with a creaky, vertical bureaucracy to occupy a primitive country with a sprawling, mountainous geography.

Afghanistan may have been lost even before the distraction of the Iraq War. For many weeks in 2003, I was embedded with a suc-cession of Army Special Forces A-teams in Afghanistan. It was often the same story. The Green Berets, operating out of small firebases, befriending the locals, proposed innovative operations that often failed to make it up through the layers of army decision-making in Kabul and Bagram Air Base. The Green Berets, working-class non-commissioned officers who typically had high school diplomas or two years of community college, were always worried about what could go wrong and often showed sensitivity to the culture in which they were immersed, which they knew they could not change much. Most had not read Greek tragedy, but their hardscrabble blue-collar lives had taught them the essence of it.

But Washington soon took over, and it preferred to conduct the war in a way it was comfortable with, rather than in a manner suited to the environment. The situation deteriorated. Innovative

---

commanders emerged and applied principles of counterinsurgency. Fate was completely rejected and replaced with human agency. In part it was a heroic effort. But the gods – in this case, the intractable Afghan propensity for weak and corrupt central government – proved insurmountable, and the Afghan soldiers we trained had too little to fight for, compared to their fellow Afghans fighting for religion. Afghanistan, like civil-war-torn Sierra Leone, like post-Saddam Iraq, offered the principles of a classical education.

Chapter 5

ORDER CREATES PERPETUAL CONFLICT
BETWEEN LOYALTY TO THE FAMILY
AND LOYALTY TO THE STATE

In 1993, I was hitchhiking from Togo westward to the Ivory Coast, negotiating one roadblock after another manned by soldiers demanding bribes. Finally, near the end of my journey, I crossed into the Ivory Coast. Now I was in a ramshackle bus. It was suddenly stopped by a group of ragged armed men without uniforms who demanded that the passengers line up to have their belongings checked. It was clearly a shakedown. Arguments broke out between the passengers and the armed men. Several groups formed and I spotted a taxi a short distance away. I made an impulsive decision to run for it. I leapt into the taxi, which sped away toward Abidjan, the capital. Within an hour I was back within a semblance of order in the country's largest city. The Ivory Coast would later descend into nearly a decade of anarchy before gradually recovering.

There is no humane alternative to order. Ask the Afghans, who in the mid-1990s turned to the Taliban out of desperation following several years of anarchy in which various mujahideen groups fought for control of the country. Without order, civilization is impossible.

Yet order is often oppressive, stultifying, cruel. There are many examples of cruel orders, ancient and modern, where the state is so overpowering that it sometimes forces individuals to be disloyal to their own families. There are also many cases where an individual insincerely expresses undying loyalty to an oppressive state in order to protect his or her family. Yet in both situations, the conflict is not about the good versus the bad but about one good versus another good: loyalty to the existing order, which promotes stability however unjust at times, against loyalty to family, which is almost always a good. Civilization and social orders can exist and flourish only when both loyalties are prevalent. Tribal loyalties, while looked down upon as irrational by the post-Enlightenment West, are also a good in themselves, as St. Augustine suggested: although tribes arise from blood relations, they are a form of social cohesion.[1]

Hegel understood Greek tragedy as about the tension between an ethical life lived within a larger, defined community and one lived within one's blood relations. Both goods are legitimate, but sometimes they are antagonistic, leaving the protagonist no option but to do wrong, whatever he or she decides.

Sophocles' *Antigone,* written in 441 BC, was for Hegel the definitive tragedy about the conflict between family and state loyalties. He called it "the most excellent, the most satisfying work of art."[2] There is something indescribably austere, stately, and horrible about the play, with its air of mathematical certainty and doom.

Antigone, the daughter of the blinded Oedipus, who guided and cared for him until his death, is now burdened with the task of interring one of her brothers, Polyneices. Polyneices and his brother Eteocles killed each other in a duel over which of them would rule Thebes. Their uncle, Creon, inherited the throne and buried Eteocles with honors, but because Polyneices allied with foreign princes to invade Thebes, Creon has deemed him a traitor and left his body to rot on the open plain. Polyneices, moreover, was vicious and hedonistic. Still, he was Antigone's brother, and she is bound by blood to bury him. The heroine is caught between family custom and political decree. For Hegel, such choices can be "turning points" in history, transitions between one kind of order and another.[3] This is where the personal, family drama intersects the destinies of city-states and empires.

Antigone makes her choice. She begins to bury Polyneices. Later, Creon's guards discover that someone has covered Polyneices' remains with some dirt and, suspecting Antigone, they drag her before the king. Creon accuses her of breaking the law. Antigone says there is a higher law of justice that dwells with the gods. Though Creon is consumed by pride, a principal cause of tragic outcomes, he nevertheless only wants peace and order in his kingdom. He believes it would be best just to hide the matter and see Antigone married to his son, Haemon. That way his rule would be legitimized among the elite of the kingdom and he would not be loathed. But Antigone does not yield. Her first loyalty is to her brother, whom she must finish burying. As Bowra succinctly puts it, "The burial of Polyneices is demanded by the gods and refused by a man."[4] Because she puts the family ahead of the city, Creon is forced to sentence her to death.

Creon defends his logic, and the reason for state power in general:

> For the worst of evils is indiscipline.
> Cities it ruins, and leaves homes desolate,
> And breaks in rout leagued armies of allies.
> Where men succeed, it is obedience,
> Above all else, that saves them.
> So now, it is ours to uphold the cause of order . . .[5]

Sophocles draws a direct line between Antigone's refusal to obey her king and the prospect of anarchy. To moderns, living under thick strata of bureaucratic authority, this fear might seem overblown. But in the ancient world, only the fear of anarchy maintained authority. It is a useful lesson to keep in mind for our own times, given the specter of disorder not only within individual states like the Ivory Coast or Afghanistan, but in the world system at large.

Yet Antigone's answer can only be:

What law of god have I transgressed? And yet
How can I look, alas, for help divine?[6]

This is the ultimate cri de coeur, a reason for religion in the first place: the need to do right out of both love and principle, even when there is no earthly reward or acknowledgment of the fact.

Creon consigns Antigone to a cave with a day's worth of food. Tiresias, the blind seer, warns against this decision. And so after a while, the torn Creon finally relents. He goes and buries Polyneices and is now ready to pardon Antigone. But Antigone has already hanged herself. Both Haemon, her betrothed, and Eurydice, Creon's wife, then kill themselves out of grief. Greek tragedy leaves no path of escape in this orderly, almost mechanical universe. The violence can seem almost pointless.

But as with so many Greek tragedies, the moral truth of the story is complex. "Antigone knows that the laws of the gods are the basis of human order and morality," Bowra notes.[7] But the tyrant Creon, too, has right on his side. He is devoted to the city over ties of kin. He regards the earth as political territory, not subject to blood ties. He stands for control over nature, whereas Antigone's obsession with burying her brother indicates a "fusion and sympathy" with nature. Creon stands for the rational; Antigone for the emotional. "It is part of the tragic situation of the play that neither house nor city proves a center of civilized values," observes the late Harvard classics professor Charles Segal.[8]

As stark and austere as Sophocles is, he is not given to black-and-white solutions. He is moral without being moralistic; intense, but without passion. For again, passion is often the enemy of analysis. Passion is easy when those who are consumed by it — columnists, for instance — do not struggle under the weight of bureaucratic responsibility.

But then we have Euripides, who engages more our modern sensibilities precisely because of his concern for the effect of war on families. Whereas Aeschylus and Sophocles leave no way out of the dilemmas they raise, indicating that tragedy requires us to accept a vastly imperfect world that is at the same time infused with awe, Euripides hints at fighting for a better world, because there are cruelties we simply should not accept. He is more vivid, less archaic, and more approachable than Aeschylus and Sophocles. Euripides among all the tragedians is the friend of the humanitarian community. This may be why some critics feel Euripides marks the end of tragedy in its purest, most uncompromising form.

Euripides wrote *Iphigenia at Aulis* shortly before his death in 406 BC. It is likely that the play had several authors. Like *Antigone*, it is about the conflict between duty to family and duty to the state. The setting is Aulis in Boeotia, where a Greek fleet of a thousand ships is assembled, ready to sail to Troy to besiege the enemy city at the start of the Trojan War. But the fleet is stranded because of a strange lack of wind. The prophet Calchas informs the Greek commander, Agamemnon, that the goddess Artemis is angry with him and has stalled the winds. To appease Artemis, Calchas tells Agamemnon that he must sacrifice his eldest daughter, Iphigenia. Agamemnon is horrified at what the seer tells him he must do. Yet he must consider it, given that his assembled troops have grown restless waiting on the beach and are now literally baying for blood. So he sends a letter to his wife, Clytemnestra, telling her to bring Iphigenia to Aulis, where she is to wed the Greek warrior Achilles. However, Agamemnon soon has second thoughts and sends another letter to his wife telling her to ignore the first letter. But the second letter is intercepted by Agamemnon's brother, Menelaus, who is angry with Agamemnon over his hesitancy and change of heart. It is the abduction of Menelaus's wife, Helen, by the Trojans that incited the war to begin with. The brothers argue. Agamemnon pleads,

> I will not kill my own children; I will not offend against
> justice so that you may prosper by avenging yourself on your
> harlot wife, while night and day consume me with tears for
> my lawless deeds, my crimes against my own children![9]

Iphigenia and Clytemnestra appear in the military camp at Aulis, having gotten the first but not the second letter. Agamemnon is devastated:

> It is a terrible thing for me to carry out this act, my wife, and
> terrible if I do not . . . You see the size of this naval prepara-
> tion, the scores of Greek warriors, armed in bronze, for whom
> there will be no voyage to conquer Ilium's towers and level
> Troy's glorious foundations, unless I sacrifice you [Iphigenia]
> as Calchas the prophet prescribes. A passionate desire rages in
> the Greek army to sail with all speed against that foreign land

> . . . These men will kill my young daughters in Argos, as well
> as you and me, if I ignore the command of the gods' oracles.[10]

Here is the true pathos of high office. Agamemnon has all the authority, yet his choices are truly awful, even as he is threatened and beleaguered by those formally under his command. He can only envy the common man and soldier, who has no such burdens. The paradox of power is to be in charge but not fully in control.

As if to drive home the point, Clytemnestra, fearful of what the soldiers under her husband's command might do if Agamemnon does not sacrifice Iphigenia, says,

> Yes, a mob is a curse and a fearful thing.[11]

Clytemnestra then asks Achilles, who vows to defend Iphigenia, if someone would actually lay hands on her girl. Achilles responds,

> Men past numbering . . .[12]

In the end, Iphigenia herself resolves the issue by going nobly to her death:

> Mother, as I reflected, I am resolved to die . . . On me depend
> the voyage of the fleet . . . with me it lies to stop barbarians
> carrying off our women from prosperous Greece . . . All this I
> will achieve by my death, and my fame as the liberator of
> Greece shall prove blessed. . . . You bore me to be the child of
> all Greeks, not yours alone. Countless men . . . will dare to do
> brave deeds against the enemy . . . shall my one life stand in
> the way of this? Where would lie the justice in this?[13]

Here we have a conclusion whereby a young and innocent life is sacrificed for the cold machinations of the state and an ambitious seer. And yet the state, with all its monstrous imperfections, must exist to monopolize violence so that humanity is not defined by endless revenge killing. The state rescues us from the primitive. Euripides knows the world cannot be fixed, but he is committed to making us feel the world's pain.

The fact that the state should monopolize the use of violence rescues us from the worst of fates: anarchy. But we should not turn our eyes from the bloodthirstiness of the state itself. I do not mean just the famously industrialized tyrannies of the twentieth century, Nazi Germany and Stalin's Soviet Union, which took state power to obscene lengths. I mean something more mundane: the state or empire in its primitive form, whose values could be little better than the Hobbesian anarchy which it was meant to suppress. The very tension between state and family loyalties, while unresolvable, helps keep the state within reasonable moral limits.

In *Coriolanus,* one of Shakespeare's last tragedies, set in the earliest years of the Roman Republic, we see patriotism take on a particularly gory, nihilistic cast, in which family love at times nearly disappears. Though there have been brave mothers and lovers throughout history, there is something terrifying about Coriolanus's mother, Volumnia, saying that if her son were her husband, she "should freelier rejoice" in his absence, wherein he won honor on the battlefield, "than in the embracements of his bed."[14] She goes on to say that if she had twelve sons, she would rather have "eleven die nobly for their country than one voluptuously surfeit out of action."[15] Patriotic mothers may accept the death of their sons in battle, but most buckle under the weight of such misfortune.

They never rejoice in it or are wholly committed to it. Volumnia is different.

Coriolanus himself is grim, bloody, stubborn, and proud, with unbridled anger at the whole notion of humanity. There is something deeply archaic about him. He appears to have no inner life, spiritual or secular. He constitutes the sum of an embattled state and culture bred only for war, and Volumnia's heartlessness further reveals it. The conflict between loyalty to the family and to the state does not humanize these characters like it does in Greek tragedy. Shakespeare is describing a warrior state that almost smothers humanity. *Coriolanus,* written in the first decade of the seventeenth century, seems more distant to us than *Antigone* and *Iphigenia,* written 2,000 years earlier. Coriolanus's mother cries for Rome, and only at the end of the play, after Coriolanus is killed by Rome's enemies, the Volscians, does she beg for peace. The tragedy lies in the fact that both mother and son realize their proper loyalties too late.

"There is no soul-searching in the Rome of *Coriolanus* because there are no fully developed souls to be searched," writes the Shakespeare scholar Paul A. Cantor. There is only "the grandeur of statues." Harold Bloom, quoting the early nineteenth-century English critic William Hazlitt, says that Coriolanus lives only within "the insolence of power."[16] Clearly, power is not something to idolize but something we must acknowledge as necessary.

The power inherent in the state creates a clash of opposites: between loyalty to the state and a personal loyalty to the family. The genius of the Greeks and of Shakespeare is to show the unity of these opposites through suffering. What the characters in *Coriolanus* suffer at the end of the play is what the characters in *Antigone* and *Iphigenia* suffer throughout—the Greek protagonists literally *live* this clash. And it is this clash in which reposes the fact that for the state to be the state it must monopolize the use of force. There is no way out.

The crux of the problem is when the state becomes so tyrannical that it loses legitimacy, challenging it can be a moral act. Camus, remember, said that even at that point, the rebel who challenges a tyrannical state must have an alternative order of government in mind to implement, or his rebellion loses legitimacy, since anarchy is worse than tyranny. We saw this dilemma played out during the Arab Spring in Syria and Libya, where tyrannical orders were rightfully challenged, but where the result was the deeper hell of anarchy, because the rebels were incapable of establishing alternative orders. And more pointedly, though Saddam Hussein's regime in Iraq had no contemporary rival in terms of brutality save perhaps for North Korea, challenging him was immoral unless there was a specific and well-thought-out plan in place to install a more enlightened alternative regime. Again, there is often no way out of this dilemma.

Chapter 6

THE STATE BECOMES THE
WELLSPRING OF AMBITION

Most men are not drawn to commit violence, but we are attracted to it. The closer men are to the use of force — especially the closer they are bureaucratically to it — the more fulfilled they become. To specialize in war studies, and better yet to work in a place like the Pentagon, is a substitute for engaging directly in combat. Women, too, now engage in combat and fill many executive and administrative positions in the military. But warfare has historically been the province of men and a focus of their ambitions. In the modern era, because it has been the state that generally monopolizes the legitimate use of violence, competition for bureaucratic power has been fierce.

In Washington, competition among men and women for a limited number of high government positions resembles a blood sport. Once someone attains such a position, his or her luck may still run out, and their association with a war or a policy gone wrong may mean they are humiliated forever; officials associated with the Iraq War have tendered the best example. Nevertheless, power is hard to resist. In my experience, people will gladly exchange a lucrative business career for a badly paying government job, in which *the call to serve* may mask other objectives. It is particularly when war is involved, or at least contemplated, that personal rivalries become fiercest, because of both the high stakes and the taste of violence in the air. High principle can be a guise for deeper motives. Even prophets are corrupted by ambition, as Agamemnon, in the throes of agony about the fate of Iphigenia, suspects of the seer Calchas.[1]

The Greeks would say that because people must ultimately come into conflict with the gods, humiliation by fate and other unsurmountable forces is inevitable. Tragedy, in the Greek view, has its roots in human strength and talent, which make the gods jealous, so that it is the very best among us who succumb to tragedy. Contrarily, Shakespeare creates tragedy not out of human strength but out of weakness: the ambitions and instincts we can't control.[2] Ambition makes us forget our origins — the place from where we came — and therefore disorients us, as Brutus explains in his allusion to "young ambition's ladder."[3]

Some of the most memorable lines in *Julius Caesar* involve the irresistible pull of ambition, which, like jealousy, is one of the defining motives of behavior, especially among governing elites. "Yond Cassius has a lean and hungry look, He thinks too much: such men are dangerous," Caesar famously worries.[4] He reads Cassius's mind well. As Cassius says of Caesar, "Why, man, he doth bestride the narrow world / Like a Colossus, and we petty men / Walk under his huge legs and peep about / To find ourselves dishonorable graves."[5] *Why should Caesar's name be sounded more than ours,* Cassius goes on to ask.

Character is everything in the end, rising above knowledge and expertise. I have seen this over and over again in Washington, to the point that when someone is appointed a secretary of state or defense, I seek to review not their résumé but what their judgment would be in a crisis. Dick Cheney, Donald Rumsfeld, and Paul Wolfowitz all had long and stellar records in public service. Both Cheney and Rumsfeld had previously been successful defense secretaries by the time they assumed office in the younger Bush administration. Wolfowitz had served successfully as an undersecretary of defense, an assistant secretary of state, and an ambassador to a major country, Indonesia. But résumés deceived, since it was all about character and judgment at a specific moment—immediately following 9/11.

The Greeks have their limits on this question. Odysseus is honest or dishonest, trickster or not, Sophocles repeatedly tells us, as the gods or the situation demand.[6] The representation of personality as a moral or immoral agent actually begins with Shakespeare. This, Harold Bloom believes, is why "the worship of Shakespeare" should be considered the Western "secular religion . . . our mythology."[7]

And Shakespeare brings us to a critical factor in political behavior: the matter of speed, of pacing. Conscience is the enemy of action, Hamlet implies.[8] Not to act is to vegetate. In *Julius Caesar*, Brutus says that between the decision to do a "dreadful thing" and the beginning of the action itself occurs a vast and complex interior drama, a mental "insurrection" that determines the character of the individual and the course of events.[9] Most people hesitate and eventually back down from taking decisive action, but Macbeth stands in opposition to this. His power of relentless anticipation is unsurpassed in all literature. Macbeth is the opposite of Brutus (and, of course, of Hamlet), who methodically consults his conscience before acting: Brutus, unlike Cassius, is consumed less by ambition than by fear of what the dictator Caesar may become. Yet because Macbeth is full of anticipation and rarely hesitates, there is a diabolical speed to his actions, and to the play to which he gives his name. Everything happens quickly in *Macbeth*. There is little reflection or self-awareness. Speed is the enemy of an inner life and conscience, with all of its conflicts of the soul. Macbeth lives in the moment with a particular animal intensity, somewhat like Dostoevsky's Raskolnikov, though one is a thane and the other a pauper (and though Macbeth has little self-awareness and Raskolnikov has so much of it that he is given to monomania). Macbeth's are the quick movements of the jungle.

Whereas Macbeth is all action, Lady Macbeth is all will: "unsex me," she says, and "fill me . . . Of direst cruelty."[10] Theirs is a great love that makes me think of other violent dictators and national leaders whom I wrote about as a journalist, men who were inseparable from the dark, driving ambitions of their wives: Nicolae Ceausescu of Romania, Zviad Gamsakhurdia of Georgia, and Slobodan Milosevic of Yugoslavia. They ruled with their wives as couples, however unofficially. Of course, the classic twentieth-century leader with an ambitious wife was Juan Perón of Argentina. Without ambition, men and women cannot seek to improve the world.

And yet ambition can be interwoven with bad judgment and disaster. Putin's historical ambition was to finally unite Ukraine with the Russian motherland. And look what happened.

All consequential human decision rests on a knife's edge. What stands out particularly, as we know from *King Lear*, is how the most personal of issues can bring down a state or kingdom. This is why high political and diplomatic drama is ultimately Shakespearean, that is, filled with the most personal of motives. *Lear* is the ultimate family and political tragedy: the worse because the two are intertwined. Where there should be order and custom and succession, there is only chaos and desolation upon Lear's abdication of authority. After *Lear*, Harold Bloom suggests, authority and kingship in the Western world were never quite the same. There is a choking sadness in *Lear* that is not quite matched by Shakespeare's other tragedies. As George Steiner writes, *Lear* offers no solution to "the twist of the net which brings down the hero," since "the mesh is woven into the heart of life."[11] There is no orderly mechanism by which Lear can retire from the throne, even though he is wracked by age. And his daughters, save for Cordelia, are corroded by ambition and cunning. Tragedy, which finds meaning in all the horror of life, is a triangle formed by ambition, violence, and anarchy.

Antony decries the chaos that emanates from the murder of Caesar: "this foul deed shall smell above the earth / With carrion men groaning for burial."[12] When ambition leads to chaos, that is the quintessence of tragedy. Topple a leader and see what happens: it rarely turns out well. I knew intimately the horror of Saddam Hussein's rule in Iraq as a reporter there in the years before the world turned its attention to him — in 1986 I had my passport confiscated for ten days by regime authorities before they would allow me to embed with a faction of Kurdish fighters supported by Saddam against Iran. I was terrified this time and all the times I was in Iraq, and wanted Saddam gone. And I was ambitious. Even though I had warned in print that Iraq could fall into chaos in a post-Saddam era, the very shock of 9/11, coupled with the recent triumphs of the U.S. military in the 1990s' Balkan interventions and the first Gulf War, convinced me that a historical moment was now at hand to remove the Middle East's worst tyrant and erect a better, more humane form of order. How many failed wars begin with grand ambition that later gives way to deep wounds? The only way to escape ambition is through fear. Not personal fear, like the kind I knew in Iraq, but divine fear of larger forces at work. Putin had no such fear before his invasion of Ukraine. Such fear holds out the greatest hope for warning us about the danger ahead. Anxious foresight is also a requirement for moral action.

Chapter 7

AMBITION AND THE STRUGGLE AGAINST TYRANNY AND INJUSTICE

Aeschylus may or may not have written *Prometheus Bound*, a play so stark and jaw-dropping that the suffering it depicts is like the first pain ever felt in the universe. It shows how the Greeks saw the dark side of their own gods. Prometheus, who has given fire and the arts to man and who can foresee the future, is chained to a rock in the Caucasus on Zeus's orders, where a "blood-red eagle" continually tears at his liver. What can he do! As he says,

> None can do battle with Necessity.
> Yet such a fate — I cannot speak of it,
> Cannot keep silence! — yoked as I am to sorrow,
> For that privilege of power I gave to men . . .[1]

And the chorus grieves at Zeus's tyranny around the world:

> For with laws of His own, most hateful, this Zeus new-glorified
> Goads at the old Gods fallen with the spear-point of His pride.
> And a voice of lamenting replies from all the earth . . .[2]

"But nothing, no threat, no torture, could break Prometheus," Edith Hamilton notes. "His name has stood through all the centuries, from Greek days to our own, as that of the great rebel against injustice and the authority of power."[3] This is why Camus calls Prometheus "the first rebel."[4] And yet, as much as this or that rebel suffers, he might take some solace from the righteousness of his cause and the romance often attached to it. Rebels are beloved by literary, artistic, and journalistic elites. They can do no wrong, since they uphold ideals without having the burden of bureaucratic responsibility, which always complicates matters, requires disagreeable compromises, and leads to unintended consequences. Freedom fighters do not have to bargain or make concessions and thus can remain pure in their ideals. The tyrant, on the other hand, be it Zeus or a modern dictator, or even a democratically elected American president, labors under the weight of having to govern and cause suffering by choosing one good over another good. Thus even a good tyrant is rarely beloved. But as Robert Browning writes, referring to Agamemnon, the tyrant is also to be pitied, "Treading the purple calmly to his death/While round him . . . Pile the dim outline of the coming doom."[5] I once interviewed a nephew of the Romanian dictator Nicolae Ceausescu, who told me his uncle "always looked worried, preoccupied. He could not live in the moment." Indeed, "the tyrant knows that all are his enemies, and thus he must try if possible to satisfy the needs of those around him or else increase the risk of a horrible fate."[6]

The greater and more intense the tyranny, the greater the fear and loneliness of the dictator himself. I saw Nicolae Ceausescu in person once close-up, in Bucharest at a Romanian Communist Party congress in the mid-1980s. He spoke for several hours uninterrupted. Both before and after his speech, the hall shook with mass applause, with people shouting, "Ceau-se-scu, Ceau-se-scu . . . " They stayed on their feet chanting until he abruptly gave the signal to stop. For anyone to stop chanting before the others risked arrest and possibly worse. Fear was thick in the air. And yet as his nephew suggested, Ceausescu himself lived with fear. All those people in the great hall, and many more outside, would turn against him the moment they sensed any weakness on his part, which is what happened on Christmas 1989, leading to his and his wife's swift execution. The long lines at dawn for stale bread in the freezing winter, the lines for fuel, the peasants bused-in from the countryside to demonstrate in his honor, the veritable slave labor camps in the snowy mud of eastern Wallachia, and the other monstrosities of his rule, all of which I witnessed during many visits to Romania in the last decade of the Cold War, triggered simmering hatred on the part of the population. In a regime that relied for its existence on its citizens' fear and mutual isolation, nobody lived in more fear and isolation than the dictator himself. People kept their heads bowed for decades in Romania, until they suddenly bared their teeth.

The tyrant cannot subdue human nature, and it is in that nature to revolt. Man is prodigious. If he can overcome the natural world, he can overcome tyranny. "He has a way against everything, and he faces nothing that is to come without contrivance," chants the chorus in *Antigone*, in the famous "Ode to Man."[7] Humans, not gods, make fate, even as the clashing and interwoven ambitions of infinite multitudes make fate indecipherable.

That is the conundrum of existence.

And always there has been the certainty of death, made worse by the fact that for a long period during the declining years of paganism and before widespread Christianity, there was little real belief in an afterlife. It is this certainty that adds heroic context to the

—

struggles of the rebel and the tyrant both. Consider the dark humor of the graveyard scene in *Hamlet*. With a few spare lines, Shakespeare reveals the full measure of human greatness. Hamlet: "That skull had a tongue in it and could sing once." Hamlet again: "Alexander died, Alexander was buried, Alexander returneth to dust; the dust is earth; of earth we make loam; and why of that loam whereto he was converted might they not stop a beer barrel?"[8] Bones, dust, that is where it all leads. But while death – oblivion – is a certain fate, Hamlet won't let himself off the hook. His agency resides in his conscience, and in that lies the whole magnificence of history. Schopenhauer puts it best: Man "discovers adversaries everywhere, lives in continual conflict and dies with sword in hand."[9] ✓

That is to say, humanity is ambitious. Obviously, there is a good side to ambition, of which there are a plethora of examples. Political and economic development is impossible without ambition. Well-designed and functioning states harness ambition; whereas hard authoritarian regimes stifle it. It is usually through sheer personal ambition that we shape and improve the world. Even if the state is unjust, it nevertheless requires ambition – always buttressed by fear! – to challenge authority.

It is the right oscillation between courage and fear that leads to better outcomes in statecraft. Courage alone, aided by ambition, can result in irresponsible catastrophe, whereas fear by itself immobilizes policymakers. It was fear of another unnecessary world war that motivated Chamberlain at Munich. I write these lines aware that the challenges ahead for the United States are momentous. At the end of the day, Afghanistan and Iraq were limited, imperial wars from which America, with its vast and resource-rich continental geography, guarded by oceans, can recover. The casualties it suffered there were substantially less, by several multiples, than its casualties in Korea and Vietnam, from which America recovered to win the Cold War. But now there is a tense rivalry among three nuclear powers, the United States, China, and Russia, states that are also armed with immense stores of precision-guided weapons and frightening cyber capabilities. The level and quality of misjudgments that obtained in Afghanistan and Iraq would in this new era lead the world to catastrophe. Washington policymakers must henceforth get the balance between fear and ambition just right, as did our policymakers during long stretches of the Cold War.

This was particularly true of Eisenhower, the first president with a vast nuclear arsenal at his disposal, who nevertheless rejected advice from his counselors to use those weapons to America's advantage in several crisis situations, thereby setting a precedent for the coming decades. In 1953, Eisenhower rejected fighting for outright victory in Korea and settled for an armistice instead. His "middle way" in strategy was an organic outgrowth of a steely, well-grounded character and personality. He had run for president in order to save the Republican Party and the country from the isolationism of Senator Robert Taft and the crazed anti-communism of Senator Joseph McCarthy. He chose not to bail out the French militarily after their catastrophic failure at Dien Bien Phu in Vietnam in 1954 out of fear of involvement in a land war in Asia, and not to intervene against the Soviets after they crushed the Hungarian Revolution in 1956 because he knew just how fragile was the thermonuclear standoff between the United States and the Soviet Union. In hindsight, the 1950s might seem dull and peaceful, but that is only because of Eisenhower's constructive pessimism. Having commanded the invasion of Normandy, he was governed by fear as well as ambition.

Chapter 8

WAR AND ITS HORRORS

When I think of my experiences as an embedded journalist in the wars of Iraq and Afghanistan, I recall these lines from Aeschylus's *Agamemnon*:

> For if you knew our hardships! — our rough quarters,
> Ill bedded on our galleys' crowded gangways . . .
> Or, on the Trojan shore (more hateful still!),
> To live encamped beneath a hostile rampart,
> Drenched with the constant curse of rain from Heaven,
> And dews of the field, that swarmed our clothes with vermin![1]

It isn't merely the obvious danger of being killed or wounded that makes war horrible; it is the unrelenting, groaning fear of being so, mixed with extreme physical discomfort that never lets up, and which you know will be the same, day after day. The extremes of weather, the hard ground on which you sleep, the inability to wash and attend to bodily needs, the acrid smells, the sensory deprivations, the really bad, monotonous food, all combine with the regularity of close-quarters violence to make war unimaginably loathsome. While the criminality of teenage soldiers was something I had already experienced in West Africa in the early 1990s, it was the First Battle of Fallujah in Iraq in April 2004 that made me permanently fearful of advocating war.

In Fallujah I was terrified the whole time, and I was only able to bury my fear by incessantly writing in my reporter's notebook about what I saw and heard. And what I saw and heard was the chaos of gun and artillery fire coming constantly from several directions, mixed with the dust and filth of the surroundings, that went on not for minutes or hours even, but for days: days that seemed to drag on like years, and were the intense summation of what I had been experiencing with the Marines for weeks already in Iraq's Anbar province. And that, in turn, was a much further intensification of what I had experienced with Army Special Forces teams in eastern and southern Afghanistan some months earlier.

War, even when it is relatively clean, with few or no civilian casualties, and fought by honorable people, is still absolute hell. Only those who have never experienced war have the luxury of advocating it with a clean conscience.

As for equating war with honor, Falstaff in Shakespeare's *Henry IV, Part 1* famously lets loose on that delusion, with his usual humor-laced seriousness:

> Can honour set to a leg? No. Or an arm? No. Or take away the
> grief of a wound? No. Honour hath no skill in surgery then?
> No. What is honour? A word. What is in that word honour?
> What is that honour? Air. A trim reckoning! Who hath it? He

that died a-Wednesday. Doth he feel it? No. Doth he hear it? No.[2]

In short, to idealize violence, whatever the circumstances, is both monstrous and naive. But while Aeschylus, Sophocles, and Euripides all realize this, Aeschylus and Sophocles are concerned mainly with the effects of violence on the state and society, while Euripides bores down on its effects on the individual. In that, he harbors an original spirit of disgust and revolt. He holds power to account. Thus there is a distinctively modern layer of argumentation in his plays. As F. L. Lucas suggests, Euripides was among the first writers in history "to transcend the bounds of country and become a good citizen of the world."[3] Sophocles' words and thoughts may be finely chiseled, but it is the plays of Euripides that have left an irreducible imprint on my memory — particularly after my several visits to war-torn Iraq and Afghanistan.

Of course, the problem remains that war is sometimes unavoidable — since to shirk from it would directly threaten the national interest and leave the world in the hands of those who would create a more brutal and repressive order than you would. Therefore, it becomes necessary to inculcate in citizens an absolute fear of war, so they know that the times when war is appropriate are exceedingly rare. The two things that can do this are literature and experience: the actual experience of war and the literature that recreates it. None surpass Euripides in this regard.

Euripides becomes doubly important because in Vietnam and Iraq, the United States failed the test of knowing when to go to war. In addition, because there has been an all-volunteer military for two generations now, few have had the experience of combat and combat training that instills a visceral seriousness about war, making literature like Euripides' all the more necessary. Otherwise, in the minds of the commentariat, quite a few of whom have many degrees and too little life experience, war is made light of, every year becomes 1939, and every adversary is Hitler.

Like many Athenians, Euripides originally was horrified at Spartan militarism and saw the justness of the Peloponnesian War. But by the second decade of the conflict, he was evidently growing disillusioned, and what finally turned his stomach was the Athenian forces' massacre of civilians on the small south Aegean island of Melos in 416 BC. What happened was this: following several raids that had failed to make Melos renounce its ancestral ties to Sparta and submit to Athens, the Athenians sent a substantial force against the island. According to Thucydides' imagined dialogue between the Melians and the Athenians, the Melians insisted that independence and neutrality were their right. The Athenians responded that the only right in this world rested in military force, and they would seem weak if they didn't exercise it. Then they killed all the Melian men and enslaved all the women and children. Euripides' response to the atrocity was his play of the following year, *Trojan Women*.

It is a play with a cinematic bitterness that documents the awful human consequences of the Greek victory over Troy: and as such recalls the dust-strewn, fly-blown Middle Eastern warscapes of today, as well as the harrowing pictures of Goya.[4] The Trojan Queen Hecuba witnesses her daughter and daughter-in-law made slaves and concubines of the Greeks, while another daughter is sacrificed on the grave of Achilles, even as her small grandson is thrown from the walls of Troy to his death. An entire city and people have just been destroyed, and this is all communicated through the voices of several individually memorable women, once wealthy and powerful, and now reduced to helplessness. This is what makes Euripides so modern: he has transferred his bitterness at the Athenian violence against the civilians at Melos in 416 BC to the violence against the Trojans some 800 years earlier.

There is an energy and texture to Euripides that Aeschylus, despite his archetypal quality, and Sophocles, despite his analytical incisiveness, ultimately lack. You experience it in *Trojan Women,* just as you do in *Iphigenia at Aulis* and *The Bacchae. Trojan Women* is an angry, vivid play, even though to fifth-century BC Athens, the fall of Troy was an ancient, half-mythical event that happened on distant shores.

Because the issue here is about taking responsibility in a world in which something is irremediably wrong and cannot be fixed — and that means sometimes advocating war — it is important to provide a brief description of *Trojan Women,* so that we never lose sight of war's details.

The play opens with a scene of squalid, makeshift tents set against the ruins of a captured and destroyed city, where a few women, the sole survivors, appear, including Queen Hecuba, with hair shorn and dressed in rags. She cries,

> O god, O god, whose slave shall I be?
> Where in this wide world shall I live
> My life out, doing drudgework,
> Stooped, mechanical, a less-than-
> Feeble token of the dead?
> Shall I be a guard stationed at
> Their doors? A nursemaid to their children?
> I who was once the queen of Troy?[5]

This could be the cry of any refugee from any war who has seen her station in life drop precipitously and is forced to struggle among strangers merely to survive.

Euripides universalizes war, just as he does the refugee experience:

> They were cut down, one after another,
> Though no one had been menacing their homeland,
> Raiding their borders, scaling their high-walled cities.
> And those the War God caught never again
> Got to see their children, nor had their bodies wrapped
> In winding sheets by their wives' hands.
> They all lie buried in a foreign land
> While at home it goes no better, for their wives
> Die widows, and their parents childless . . .
> A war of choice is madness . . .[6]

So speaks Cassandra, Hecuba's daughter who has the troubling gift of prophecy. "A war of choice" reflects a 2009 translation from the ancient Greek by Alan Shapiro. It clearly echoes the Iraq War, then six years old. In that case it was a war to eradicate weapons of mass destruction that did not exist. In the case of Troy, the Greeks fought only for the reputation of Helen: that is, "for one woman's sake/A woman who wasn't taken by force."[7] For that, countless lives were destroyed.

Then there is the squalid reduction of a human life set against the vast canvas of violent conflict when the widow of the slain Trojan hero Hector, Andromache, enters the stage with her son Astyanax on a rickety cart, piled high with Trojan spoils. The dead are better off than the living, she remarks, referring to the recent sacrifice of Polyxena, Hecuba's youngest daughter. When the little Astyanax is hurled by the victorious Greeks from the high walls of Troy to his death on the stony ground, war is reduced to its essence – the destruction of one innocent young life, and that of a whole family that grieves forever as a consequence. "Not even a barbarian could invent/Atrocities like this," Andromache wails.[8] Nor could the gods, Hecuba answers, for these are the crimes of men.

> So in the end the gods did nothing for us.
> Anguish and more anguish is all they ever brought.[9]

Unprotected by the gods, left to their own devices, men and women are consigned to oblivion. Annihilation is complete when the Greeks set fire to the remains of Troy. The play ends with ash and smoke and "namelessness."[10] No uplifting moral comforts the audience. There is no solace. As for stoicism, it was a philosophy originally meant for slaves, as T. S. Eliot reminds us.[11] This is the history of war through the twentieth century and into the twenty-first.

Uneasy are the policymakers who must make decisions about war and peace. Because war is so horrible, the persons with whom such choices rest are, to say the least, not to be envied. To sympathize with the victims of war is morally necessary and emotionally satisfying, but analytically easy. This, again, is at the root of why intellectuals are so self-assured even as policymakers grind their teeth at night with regrets, knowing that they will get no sympathy from the likes of Euripides.

As today in Gaza 2/2024

75

Of course, the human capacity for rationalization and evasion is inexhaustible, and intellectuals are better at it than most. How many of them have confronted the costs of their follies in the Middle East over the past twenty years? Quite a few probably, at least in the darkness of their bedrooms. But judging by their performances in print and on television, many haven't.

The Biden administration's withdrawal from Afghanistan in the summer of 2021, as incompetently planned and carried out as it was, laid bare a stark truth that twenty years of posturing by policy elites and intellectuals could not mask: the Afghan state and military were a fiction. They did not reliably exist when it counted. Despite two decades of fighting and trillions of dollars spent, in the end we had built nothing. The wars in Afghanistan and Iraq were much less significant in terms of casualties compared to Korea and Vietnam. Nevertheless, in a metaphorical sense, the abject failure of our Middle Eastern wars will live on as a caution for many years.

Chapter 9

BECAUSE WAR IS EVER-PRESENT, THE BURDEN OF POWER IS OVERWHELMING

Shakespeare's Caesar reduces bravery to its essence:

Cowards die many times before their deaths,
The valiant never taste of death but once.[1]

Perhaps the only literary figure braver than Caesar is Prometheus. Prometheus sees all the horrors ahead, knows he can do nothing about them and will endure the most painful suffering for eternity, and yet is magnificent in his resolve.

It is precisely because they can endure such suffering that the truly brave are resented by others. But as Pylades says to his cousin Orestes,

Let all men hate thee rather than the Gods.[2]

A brave man is brave, in other words, because he is true to himself; therefore he is lonely in his knowledge. Consider Hamlet,

—
77

who knows the worst truths. This makes him wise. But who would want to be him?

"I envy you your lack of understanding," Agamemnon says to his daughter Iphigenia, as he feels the awful burden of knowledge and power. "I wish I shared it!"[3] He knows that while humble men can weep and "tell the full tale of their sorrow," the man in charge, in possession of horrible truths, must keep his dignity even as he is a slave of the mob.[4]

There is a crucial difference between Agamemnon and Hamlet. While both men have knowledge, Agamemnon, as the tribal leader of the Greek forces soon to face Troy, must act, and act quickly. Hamlet can afford to ruminate. It is sometimes said that leadership requires self-deception; otherwise leaders would be unable to act. But a leader may see clearly all the harm of what he is about to do no matter what path he adopts, and still have to make a decision. He knows that the reality on the ground in a distant place is rarely black and white, and that the situation is given to mystery; yet he is forced to act as if it were black and white and there were no mystery at all. Action by definition lacks the subtlety of intellectual argument. And while the leader will be judged in hindsight, at the moment he acts he knows only the facts as they are available to him. While the evidence will be at best partial, the decisions that arise from it are irrevocable. This is why bravery is intimately connected with leadership.

Consider Shakespeare's Richard II, who is, in Harold Bloom's words, "totally incompetent as a politician and totally a master of metaphor," a bad king and leader but a subtle and eloquent poet.[5] Again, it is so much easier to be an intellectual or an artist — or a journalist — than to be a king or political leader. The loneliness of leadership is of a deeper dimension than the loneliness of the others. Journalists flatter themselves that they speak truth to power. But the

---

reality is far more complex. The truths that journalists speak aloud are not just the truths that those in power obscure, but often the truths that the powerful are very much aware of but cannot do or say anything about publicly, for fear of making the situation even worse.

Of course, all this is assuming that the leader himself has a reasonable level of awareness. Macbeth and Lady Macbeth, for example, have little capacity to discern the road they are on, or to grasp the consequences of their actions. Only when they are alone in the dark with their guilty thoughts can they do so. Lady Macbeth sleepwalks, dreaming she is washing her hands of blood. And how many modern dictators have seen Banquo's ghost? Not only is there no peace of mind for rulers like Macbeth, there is none for rulers who have simply made bad choices. King Lear, for instance, is not cruel like Macbeth, yet as his daughter Regan says, "he hath ever but slenderly known himself."[6] Lear resists self-awareness. By abdicating his authority, he suffers the very worst that nature has to offer, dying of grief at the execution of his devoted daughter. This, the most profound and heartrending of Shakespeare's tragedies, sends its audience back into the world much the wiser in its perception of how the abdication of power and responsibility, even if wrought by old age, can lead to the worst outcomes.

It is the burden of leadership that provides tragedy with many of its most searing and pivotal moments.

When we think of the burden of power, we immediately associate it with failed wars. There can be no worse burden on a leader's peace of mind than to know that he has gotten thousands of his countrymen and countless more civilians killed all for naught, with terrible political consequences for his country or kingdom or city-state. It will occupy his final thoughts as he is dying.

In this regard Americans will first think of the Vietnam War, which is sometimes compared to the Athenians' ill-fated Sicilian Expedition of the late fifth century BC, described in Thucydides' *Peloponnesian War.* Fourteen years elapsed from Athens's first foray into Sicily to its final disaster there: the same span as between the Kennedy administration's early forays into Vietnam and President Gerald Ford's final withdrawal. The United States was lured half a world away by its South Vietnamese allies, who were besieged by communist forces from North Vietnam, just as Athens was lured into Sicily by its local allies there, which were threatened by other Sicilian city-states loyal to Athens's rival, Syracuse, an ally of Sparta. Just as the Kennedy administration began with the dispatch of limited Special Operations Forces to Vietnam, a commitment that grew dramatically larger under President Lyndon Johnson to over half a million regular troops, the Athenian intervention in Sicily began with 20 ships in support of its anti-Syracusan allies and quickly grew to 100 triremes, numerous transport ships, and 5,000 hoplites. With the prestige of its entire maritime empire dependent on a military victory in far-off Sicily, Athens kept pouring in manpower. The Sicilian Expedition ended with the defeat of 40,000 Athenian troops, of whom 6,000 survived to labor in the quarries of Syracuse and be sold into slavery. The American intervention in Vietnam ended with the communist North overrunning the South, with the last Americans fleeing by helicopter from the roof of the U.S. embassy in Saigon. President Johnson died of a broken heart just before the war ended.

But there may be an even more poignant parallel example of tragic leadership emanating from the burden of power, both in the ancient Greek past and in the recent American one. The second Persian invasion of Greece under King Xerxes in 480 BC seems to foreshadow the second American war against Iraq under President George W. Bush in 2003. As usual with such comparisons, the differences are vast, yet the similarities are illuminating.

The great Persian empire was then relatively new and dynamic, having come into existence less than 100 years before Xerxes' invasion, and its heartland lay a thousand miles to the east of Greece. It was founded by Cyrus the Great, who absorbed Media and then Lydia in Asia Minor, leading to the fall of several Greek cities by the Aegean even as, to the east, Persia advanced to the borders of the Indian subcontinent. The empire seemed invincible. Cyrus was followed on the throne by Cambyses, and he in turn by Darius. According to Herodotus, Darius was in the midst of expanding his invasion of Greece by sea when he heard the news of the Athenian victory over a Persian force at Marathon in 490 BC. Nevertheless, he succeeded in subjugating other parts of Greece in Macedonia and the Cycladic Islands before he died in 486 BC. His son, Xerxes, upon ascending to the throne, immediately began preparing for a second invasion of Greece. Greece had obsessed father and son, their wars separated by a little over a decade, much as the wars against Iraq, also separated by a little over a decade, occupied the elder and younger Bushes. And whereas Darius's historical reputation was not destroyed by his war against Greece even as his son Xerxes' was, George H. W. Bush's defeat of the Iraqi army in Kuwait was a triumph, while his son's war proved to be a disaster.

"That swift expansion and abrupt disgrace of the Persian Empire [under Xerxes], even when told as sober history, have already the quality of drama," writes Yale classics professor C. John Herington.[7] Something similar may ultimately be said about George W. Bush's American empire in Iraq. Both number among history's great reversals.

The Second Persian War represents the only contemporary historical event in Greek tragedy—all the other works of the Athenian playwrights deal with distant myth. What's more, the *Persians,* produced in 472 BC and the first play written by Aeschylus, is the oldest surviving drama in the Western tradition. Aeschylus was a soldier at the Battle of Marathon, and he writes not as a historian but as someone trying to come to terms with what he witnessed. What emerges is a revelation of destiny itself, as Darius is depicted as the "successful" father of the "incompetent" Xerxes, who shatters the imperial legacy his father has bequeathed him.[8] But the caution against hubris Aeschylus provides here isn't only for the defeated Persians. It also, presciently, applies to the victorious Greeks, whose disastrous Sicilian Expedition lay just a little more than half a century in the future.

Persians opens with the home front awaiting news of their army's linear progress, assuming in advance the invincibility of their force, for recent history has taught them to expect nothing less. "This/is the flower of Persian earth/the men now gone."[9] Much the same was assumed in 2003, when the American home front followed the march to Baghdad by U.S. ground forces. The history of the first Iraq war as well as those in the Balkans had conditioned them to expect another easy triumph. In 480 BC, as in 2003, the home front initially approached the endeavor as a "holy task."[10]

But it is "all for NOTHING / into hostile Greece," where Persian soldiers "met hard deaths. The corpses/pile on Salamis and every nearby shore."[11] All the seeming advantages of the invasion force gradually crumble amid a hostile, foreign landscape.

It was some Power—
Something not human—

82

> Whose weight tipped the scales of luck
> And cut our forces down.[12]

Truly, because the miscalculation is so monumental, it must have a higher purpose, something the gods have done in order to teach humility. But it only gets worse, "till every living man was butchered." Others starved or died of thirst, reducing the Persian soldiery to prayer and beggary. Xerxes is now described at home as "the hothead" who "brought on the whole rout."[13] The chorus asks,

WHY HAVE TIMES CHANGED?[14]

Xerxes' utter incompetence, considering the greatness of his father, seems like a crime against nature. It wasn't supposed to be like this. The chorus claws at the earth as if to free Darius's spirit.

> Shah once and forever
> > come close
> > break through . . .
> Father who brought us no evil
> Darius
> > Break free[15]

Tragedy signals a sudden change in heroic fortune. There is a great yearning for more glorious times and easier, more decisive wars. But Zeus is "the Pruning Shear of arrogance" and the "grim accountant."[16]

The details can always be argued about. If only Xerxes had done this, in that instance . . . or that, in another instance. If only the younger Bush had fired Defense Secretary Donald Rumsfeld in

2004, after Bush had just been reelected and it would have been convenient to do so, rather than two years later as he did . . . how the tide might have been turned sooner . . . But it is precisely when all the details and circumstances work against you that it means something larger is at work. Beware shifting blame, though. Fate is something we do to ourselves and afterward blame the gods.

Iraq, like the war depicted in *Persians,* is mythic even though it doesn't rank in consequence alongside Xerxes' invasion of Greece or Napoleon's and Hitler's ill-fated invasions of Russia. Like Vietnam and the Sicilian Expedition, Iraq will never be forgotten. As someone who knew Iraq firsthand under tyranny and later firsthand under anarchy — and who supported the war because of that vivid experience of tyranny — I must live with that truth. Literature should not only inspire but trouble. Tragedy teaches that no one should die with a clear conscience.

Chapter 10

IMPERIAL WARS ARE DECIDED BY FATE

Democracies and republics, by allowing their citizens wide-spread participation in politics, give tangible expression to the ideal of human intervention, so the actions of individuals, not the gods, decide our fates. But as republics and democracies grow successful and become empires, so many new and vast historical forces come into play that the idea of human agency weakens, and fate again edges in. The Homeric world of individual heroes as well as the early Rome of *Coriolanus* and *Julius Caesar,* where a handful of men had outsized influence on events, were different places from the sprawling imperial domain of *Antony and Cleopatra,* with its cosmopolitan cross-currents and passing of historical ages.[1] Empire leads to universality, but also to a loss of direction and control. *Coriolanus* and especially *Julius Caesar,* evoking the time of a smaller and more republican Rome, are worlds of the here and now, whereas *Antony and Cleopatra*'s backdrop of world empire is a mystical realm of fate where intervention and restraint have been dramatically weakened. This is all captured in Harold Bloom's description of Mark Antony as a "magnificent ruin": a wasted figure whom Octavius calls the

———

"abstract" of all our faults.[2] The Greek poet C. P. Cavafy sums this up in his poem "The God Abandons Antony":

> . . . don't mourn your luck that's failing now,
> work gone wrong, your plans
> all proving deceptive – don't mourn them uselessly . . .
> go firmly to the window
> and listen with deep emotion . . .
> to the exquisite music of that strange procession,
> and say goodbye to her, to the Alexandria you are losing.[3]

The god who is abandoning Antony, exiting Alexandria with his musical procession, is according to some interpretations Bacchus (Dionysus), the god of license and chaos, who inspired Antony's indiscipline and sexual intrigue with Cleopatra. With Antony's death, the efficient soldier Octavius Caesar takes power in the Mediterranean and Rome's age of empire truly begins. The noble patriotism of the Roman Republic, with its intimacy, accountability, and human agency, is gone. Yet the universal cross-currents of civilizations, suggested in Shakespeare's last great tragedy, will only grow in influence. With tyranny on one hand and the swirl of world history on the other, as events from Britain to Persia increasingly influence Rome's new imperial destiny, there is a sense of an opaque future that humans are powerless to alter. As Mark Antony suggests, only the soothsayers know what is really happening.

Sometimes I imagine the face of Richard Holbrooke looking out that same window, listening to "the exquisite music of that strange procession," mourning the passage of a triumphant post–Cold War America and the tragic final descent into empire. Holbrooke was brilliant and dedicated beyond measure, blessed with a sonorous voice and a towering, intimidating presence, which helped him to fix specific problems on the ground in distant places. But while the world might be fixable here and there, as America strode into a larger canvas in places like Afghanistan and Iraq, that very same world proved more and more intractable, as Holbrooke discovered trying to fix Afghanistan at the time of his death.

I think the moment it became clear to me that we were no longer in control was the February 2006 bombing of the al-Askari Shrine in Samarra, Iraq, one of the holiest sites in Shia Islam. That act more than any other plunged Iraq into all-out sectarian war. Up to that point Iraq appeared arguably fixable, and our invasion possibly headed toward a decent end. But as the mosque collapsed, all hope was lost.

Suddenly Americans learned that their power to change the world was circumscribed. The world had histories and traditions that were not subject to America's own historical experience with democracy. A decade later, America gave up any credibility with which to lecture distant places about the path to better governance after it elected Donald Trump, a tawdry demagogue, as its president. Trump's effect on our domestic politics laid bare the American system's tenuousness: that rather than provide answers for distant societies, we could find some of the pathologies of those distant societies visited upon us. America's estimable civic culture might actually have been a creature of the print-and-typewriter age, when the media and public opinion were oriented toward the political center. But now the digital-video age of social media was fraying the national fabric and contributing to the rank partisanship in Washington. Rather than the national cohesion afforded by World War II and its Cold War extension, we now seemed headed into a messy, dangerous world, both foreign and domestic.

—

The journey from a republic to a world empire, which is the journey America traveled in the twentieth and early twenty-first century, means losing ourselves in what Reinhold Niebuhr called "a vast web of history, in which other wills, running in oblique or contrasting directions to our own, inevitably hinder or contradict what we most fervently desire."[4] A degree of agency has been lost. Again, we are not fully in control. That is the conundrum we now face.

Beyond the conflict in Ukraine with Russia, confronting us now is the specter of a hot war with China over Taiwan, the South China Sea, or the East China Sea; or all three at once. We shouldn't kid ourselves: even if it lasts just a few days, such a war will panic financial markets around the globe as the world's largest and most developed economies come to blows. Many could be killed and die awful deaths amid the flames of incoming projectiles; submarines might crack apart or crumble as men and women are instantly crushed by the water pressure. And don't think everything will be clear. I have been embedded on destroyers and nuclear submarines for long periods and have witnessed war games aboard, as dozens of officers and sailors stare at their computer screens in a sensory-depressed environment where every hard surface is gray and you can practically smell the heat of the liquid crystal screens: the tension here is as great as that under live fire in Iraq, as the enemy now is one click away. The fog of war is as thick at sea as in the desert. The very quantity of projectiles exchanged can cause confusion. Information systems can tell you the split-second situation of a target, but they cannot tell you the other side's intention. There have also been near-collisions at sea where, despite the naval codes of conduct, it is unclear which ship captain was supposed to yield. A Chinese move against Taiwan might be so subtle that it will not be clear until afterward whether the intention was to invade the island or merely soften up its population through disinformation campaigns that make an end run around Taiwanese sovereignty.

The failures in Iraq and Afghanistan were our obsessions for a long time. But the stakes will be infinitely higher in the future. China is only one example: the challenges of Russia and Iran as we know are others. George W. Bush is a figure of pathos, but fate could have worse in store for our future leaders.

What is fate, *moira* in Greek?

Fate is "the dealer-out of portions,"[5] or as George Steiner defines it, "unyielding destiny which maintains through its apparently blind decimations an ultimate principle of justice and equilibrium."[6] It is the "will of Zeus," not the power behind Zeus, and this makes all the difference, says Maurice Bowra, since Zeus's will is subject to occasional bending.[7]

Men yield to fate only when they are full of illusions, which they are often but not always. The predictions of the weird sisters come true not because the sisters can see the future but because they harbor an insight into Macbeth's character. It is often a single flaw in an otherwise noble character that leads to catastrophe. And that flaw is usually pride, which leads one to be a victim of illusions in the first place.[8] Thus the goal of life, as Aeschylus implies in *Choephoroe*, is to win the "favor of Zeus" through "righteousness," which involves, among other things, the casting-off of illusions.[9]

Of course, the victim of fate can sometimes be absolutely righteous in his character. Such is Oedipus, whose life, nevertheless, is a complete disaster. Oedipus is a plaything of the gods, who employ him and destroy him in order to teach humankind a lesson. There is no agency in the tale of Oedipus. In that sense it is a lowering story. And yet Oedipus's struggle to comprehend what has happened to him constitutes tragedy in its purest, most uplifting form. The effect of tragedy is like standing on a mountaintop in the thunder and driving rain, experiencing all the majesty of life through extremes of discomfort and vulnerability. And the foundation of all tragedy is fate, which by definition is cruel.

The most elegant, enviable personalities are those who understand when fate is inescapable, and give in to it with such style that they teach the rest of us how to cope. The Prince in Giuseppe Tomasi di Lampedusa's *The Leopard* is such a character. Lampedusa's evocation of fate is both luscious and sensuous, yet because of the strength of its metaphors it is at the same time the opposite of purple. Lampedusa's depiction of nineteenth-century Sicily defines tragedy with the power of the ancient Greeks.

"They were the most moving sight there," Lampedusa writes of one handsome couple, "two young people in love dancing together, blind to each other's defects, deaf to the warnings of fate, deluding themselves that the whole course of their lives would be as smooth as the ballroom floor." They are two young bodies, amorous and aroused, "destined to die." The course of their love, like that of so many others, is "flames for a year, ashes for thirty." When the scene is enlarged beyond the dancers, the reader sees a country defiled by the "violence of landscape," the "cruelty of climate," and "continual tension in everything," with seaboards reached easily by conquerors who built monuments but left no tradition of development and hard work.[10] The Prince, all-knowing, like Oedipus at the end of his life, is aware of all this. And he also knows he can ultimately do nothing about it. Sicily is like a vast and enervating jungle,

---

thick with vines, that slowly, luxuriantly strangles him. The Prince is wise but no hero.

To be wise is one thing, but to struggle against the impersonal forces of fate when defeat seems certain constitutes true greatness. Yet there is another path to true greatness, which brings us back to the story of Oedipus.

Chapter 11

FROM THE SUFFERING OF HEROES COMES
THE ESSENCE OF TRAGEDY

Sophocles was less interested in the division between good men and bad men than in differences in the degree to which men deceive themselves.[1] And no figure in Greek tragedy, or in all of human experience, knew so much and comprehended so little about himself as Oedipus, king of Thebes.[2]

Oedipus ruled a great city and vanquished a half-man, half-beast monster, the Sphinx, by deciphering one of the Sphinx's seemingly impossible-to-solve riddles. He accomplished all of this by virtue of his supreme intelligence, yet he was ignorant of the most fundamental facts about himself. He had unknowingly murdered his father, King Laius, and married his mother, Jocasta. Oedipus learns this – and who he really is – in the course of a relentless search for the causes of a plague that has nearly destroyed his city. He is fearless in his pursuit of knowledge, but when he learns the horrible truth about himself, he puts out his eyes. Blinded, he begins to see and understand the world better than when he had sight. Desolately wandering the world in rags, attended by his daughter Antigone, Oedipus is alone in the

---

blackness with only his guilty thoughts, knowing his life is a ruin. No man has suffered like this once great and rich king, yet he says to his daughters, Antigone and Ismene, "No man could give you deeper love than mine."[3]

Oedipus is heroic in the dignified way that he bears his suffering and mental torture. The gods have made an example of him in order to teach all of us never to feel secure in our prosperity or position, since tragedy can befall anyone at any time. Oedipus was a great and admired king who is now a despised pauper, yet his example manifests human dignity in the face of disaster. By searching out the truth, he has learned about his own evil and insignificance: no matter that he was a king; no matter that his crimes were committed unknowingly. Precisely because of the extent and degree of his suffering, he has achieved a certain greatness.

"A great soul makes an easy target," writes Sophocles in *Ajax*.[4] That is another fundamental aspect of tragedy. True suffering is the only way to see, to have illuminated to you some essential truth about your life and the human condition. The hero is a unique individual who is set apart from others by suffering, but who at the end sees his or her life as part of a larger design. As Shakespeare writes in *Hamlet*,

> Our wills and fates do so contrary run
> That our devices still are overblown:
> Our thoughts are ours, their ends none of our own.[5]

What we set out to accomplish is rarely what we do accomplish, since our thoughts and the actions that follow from them lead to unintended ends: this is because society has its own say, however unfair it may be. It is another feature of tragedy that self-awareness usually comes too late.

It is our very capacity for knowledge that leads to suffering, writes Schopenhauer, since obviously the more you know, the more you worry. Or as the Russians would say, *the less you know, the better you sleep.* The whole world, Schopenhauer concludes, is "a place of atonement."[6] William Wordsworth writes that throughout our lives, while actions and decisions are "transitory" because they take place in an instant, the suffering that results from those actions is "permanent."[7] Oedipus in his exile adds only this comfort: "My sufferings have taught me to endure."[8]

Yet how exactly do we endure? By knowing our place before the gods — a form of submission to the larger scheme of things. Any life, thoughtfully lived, contains an acknowledgment of failure, and with it, a deeper insight into not only ourselves but into our world and civilization. This is Oedipus's triumph. The hero at the end is purified, having reconciled himself to a supreme justice.[9] This is why *Oedipus at Colonus,* Sophocles' last play, is truly sublime.

Harold Bloom, in another context, tells us that it is only through consolation and a "sharing of grief" that "the aesthetic experience of tragedy" is manifest.[10] Mere sadness will not do, since that can be about the surface of things. Decadent people live sad lives all the time, but there is no elevation in it of the kind that tragedy requires. Sad decadence, by the way, is the theme of Ford Madox Ford's great novel about careless people who mistake appearances for reality, *The Good Soldier* (1915).

Tragedy is the very stuff of theater and ritual, showing us the cruelest side of life and nature and, according to Nietzsche, sending us back into the world "with renewed energy and reinforced psychic strength."[11]

Consider the conclusion of Dostoevsky's *Crime and Punishment:* "Tears stood in their eyes. They were both pale and thin, but in those pale, sick faces there already shone the dawn of a renewed future, of a complete resurrection into a new life. . . . They resolved to wait and endure. They still had seven years more, and until then so much unbearable suffering, and so much infinite happiness!"[12] A resurrection through love gives Raskolnikov and Sonya the courage to face his sentence of seven years of hard labor. Thus does the spirit of Christianity link up with that of the Greek gods, for they both are about the same thing: a form of submission before higher elements that give us humility, so that in being thankful to be alive, we accept what nature has wrought.

Obviously there are crimes beyond redemption, to which the Greeks, Shakespeare, and Dostoevsky have no answer. We saw enough of them in the twentieth century: perpetrated by Hitler, Stalin, Mao, and Pol Pot. And there is no letup in the twenty-first. Witness the Chinese depredations against the Turkic Uighur Muslims. Such monstrously evil crimes are neither the stuff of tragedy nor of this essay. Nevertheless, it is in the enforcement of humility before the gods that tragedy can help in the development of anxious foresight, a condition for a better world by warning us of trouble to come. To think tragically is to know that all things cannot be fixed, even as life must go on.

The political and humanitarian crises that I have witnessed firsthand or engaged with during my career as a journalist could all have been helped by anxious foresight, which requires a tragic sensibility—something that Americans, being an ahistorical people, lack. America, blessed with a resource-rich continental geography protected by vast oceans, is so geographically fortunate that even foreign policy disasters like Iraq and Afghanistan leave it virtually unscathed. The Washington elite pays too small a price for them, and this, in turn, allows the policy elite to shrug them off and go on just as before. Thus the learning curve is never steep. Even when it had already become clear that Iraq was a disaster and Afghanistan approaching a quagmire, in 2011 a significant faction of the policy elite supported toppling the regime in Libya by force – leading to another disaster. Such a pattern of behavior breeds a certain decadence, as too few close to power pay a reputational, emotional, or psychological price for their mistakes. This impedes the maturation of a tragic sensibility. The process of imperial management is bloody and sloppy, and since the end of World War II – and especially after 9/11 – empire has defined the United States' situation in the world. For example, the stunning surprise of the Iranian Revolution in 1978–79 should have come as no surprise at all, given the hatred of the Shah coupled with his declining health. The bombing of U.S. Marine barracks outside Beirut in 1983 was a likely culmination of an ill-defined mission amidst a nest of terrorist groups. The arming by the United States of the most radical mujahideen groups against the Soviets in Afghanistan naturally opened a path to 9/11. All of this, while specifically hard to predict, should have made us wiser regarding the ability of those whose lands we occupied or intervened in to bedevil our plans. To repeat, Afghanistan and Iraq were ghastly failures because of the way the forces of local history and culture vanquished American ideals of democracy. The Middle East has never been an extension of America's very specific historical experience. We never learned what the ancient Greeks knew: all things cannot be fixed, so we have to accept much of the world just as it is.

Chapter 12

THE TRUTH IS POSSESSED ONLY BY THE OLD AND THE BLIND

Tiresias, the old, blind seer, the prophet who knows better than anyone else the will of the gods, is a recurring character in Greek mythology. "Mine is the strength of truth," within which lies safety, he tells Oedipus, when an angry Oedipus, still king of Thebes, begins to face the horrible truth about who he really is.[1] Tiresias specializes in telling his listeners what they least want to hear—the very thoughts they repress. He is no god but almost serves the function of one. Just as you can't deceive the gods, you cannot deceive Tiresias. He is a replacement for one's conscience. Like Oedipus himself, old and blind at the end of his life, Tiresias bears the gift of insight precisely because he *is* blind: one kind of vision has been replaced by another; a penetrating, analytical way of seeing has replaced a superficial but often deceptive way of seeing. Blindness allows both Tiresias and Oedipus to see the world more accurately—a painful ability, since it means admitting what you don't want to admit to.

Both Tiresias and the dying Oedipus know that because everything mortal in this world decays, it is wise to think and act

---

as if you were already withered and old, even if you are still young. This will release you from vanity and pride, the enemies of good fortune and the mainstays of self-delusion. There is much to fear in this world: fortune can change not only gradually, especially as one ages and grows more prone to illness and disease, but suddenly. Oedipus, driven by Tiresias's prophecy, goes from the height of wealth and power to abject misery "in the course of a single day."[2]

By the time one is old, one has already experienced heartbreak and disappointment, and therefore wisdom is more likely to be found in the old than in the young. It is all about knowing yourself and your world. Recall the words of another Russian close in spirit to the ancient Greeks, Aleksandr Solzhenitsyn: "Tribes with an ancestor cult have endured for centuries. No tribe would survive long with a youth cult."[3] This is why the twenty-first-century Chinese, still benefitting from the residue of Eastern Confucian culture and its respect for hierarchy and the elderly, have an edge over the postmodern West, which, with its narcissistic obsession with youth, is no longer a spiritual descendant of the ancient Greeks: the very people who gave birth to Western civilization in the first place.

This is also why *Oedipus at Colonus,* about Oedipus's wanderings and arrival outside Athens in old age, has always been so highly regarded by critics. Maurice Bowra writes: "Oedipus' endurance in adversity entitles him to honor and ultimately to heroization."[4] His sustained fortitude in the face of all his difficulties with his family and kingdom, not to mention the travails of his wanderings, is respected by the gods. Once a man of pride and certainty, Oedipus becomes completed and wiser in what he knows about human existence, even if he is not rewarded for it in the physical world, where everyone lacks his depth of foreknowledge.

None are as wise as those who have suffered some great catastrophe, which can include public shame. Policymakers who have failed miserably are thus more likely to be genuinely interesting: more deeply reflective about their lives than those who have known only success. I would like to have known the post-Watergate Nixon, with his keen foreign policy instincts built on fear and thinking five steps ahead; but now armed with shame about his mistakes, his flawed character, and his dramatically reduced financial position. He wrote many serious books in his retirement, advised President Carter well on China policy and President Clinton well on Russia policy, and generally entered the public spotlight only on a serious note. This was a kind of penance and rehabilitation for a broken man.

We mature through mistakes. Mistakes help us to be fearful about what comes next. True wisdom is not to be envied.

As Sophocles writes at the end of *Oedipus the King,*

> Till man lies within his tomb,
> Never dare to call him "happy" — wait until your eyes shall see
> That beyond life's bourne he travels, touched by no calamity.[5]

And here is Sophocles in *Ajax,*

> . . . never
> allow yourself to speak arrogant
> words against the gods,
> or feel proud if your hand strikes harder
> than another's or wealth heaps higher
> around you. One day can lift up
> and bring down all human things.
> The gods favor wise restraint . . .[6]

In short, never dare to call a man lucky until he is dead. This is the famous advice that Solon provides the wealthy King Croesus of Lydia, who will come to know the bitter truth of this prophecy.[7] A constant fear of what is around the corner is the foundation stone of humility; it reduces the risk of catastrophes. Fear recognizes that choices are rarely between good and evil, since that is too easy. Crucial decisions are by their nature close calls and are often about choosing one good over another — or one evil over another. In fear rests safety. Lionel Trilling once said about Robert Frost that like Sophocles, Frost was beloved because he "could make plain the terrible things" and so give people comfort.[8]

Chapter 13

BECAUSE DIFFERENT GOODS STRUGGLE AGAINST EACH OTHER, WE HAVE CONSCIENCES

The late literary critic Tony Tanner wrote that while Orestes and other Greek heroes "pause" before they take action, in Shakespeare's *Hamlet* the pause consumes the entire play. While the ancient Greeks were, of course, not like beasts who act purely on instinct, still the distance traveled between the Greeks and the Elizabethans was vast. In between came the birth of Christianity and later the Reformation, the combination of which created a whole new landscape of conscience, particularly a guilty conscience.[1] Harold Bloom takes this point a step further, arguing that not only did the idea of a guilty conscience culminate with *Hamlet,* so, too — and more broadly — did the literary description of consciousness itself. Hamlet's mind truly encompasses the universe. The character of Hamlet is a forerunner to those in the novels of Henry James, which would come three hundred years after Shakespeare, explicate the minutiae of consciousness, and provide a bridge to the modernism of Joyce and Eliot.[2]

Guilt and conscience, which play such a large part in the modern Christian West, are central to the realm of tragedy. And because

---

there is such a thing as a guilty conscience, there is also evil, which requires one to deliberately overcome one's conscience. The notion of good and evil is far more developed in Shakespeare (as well as in Dostoevsky, Conrad, and others) than it is in the Greeks.

When we read Bloom and other Shakespeare scholars, it almost seems as if Shakespeare – rather than the writers of the Bible – invented evil. Iago, for example, is a much more developed depiction of Satan than anything the Bible. He practically *is* Satan. Just as Satan was passed over by God, Iago, a Venetian soldier, is passed over by the nobleman Othello, who, just as God was to Satan, is the universe and creation itself to Iago. Few characters in all of literature are as purely evil as Iago, who combines analytical brilliance with a complete lack of concern for moral consequences. Plotting against the good Desdemona and her equally sincere husband Othello, Iago declares,

> When devils will the blackest sins put on,
> . . . I'll pour this pestilence into his ear:
> That she repeals him for her body's lust;
> And by how much she strives to do him good,
> She shall undo her credit with the Moor:
> So I will turn her virtue into pitch,
> And out of her own goodness make the net
> That shall enmesh them all.[3]

Iago, the most creative mind in the play, exists only to scheme. He is brave, daring, shameless. Disinformation, misrepresentation, and modern terrorism all find their literary and aesthetic origin with him.[4] Russian president Vladimir Putin, in his bottomless cynicism and deviousness, parallels Iago. There exists a suspicion that the

1999 Russian apartment block bombings in Moscow and other cities, officially blamed on Chechen terrorists, were in fact carried out by Russia's own intelligence services in order to facilitate Putin's rise to power while general fear gripped Russia. If true, it would have been an act truly in the spirit of Iago. As one would expect, Iago is nothing if not sardonic. He says,

> There is more sense in that [a bodily wound] than in reputation. Reputation is an idle and most false imposition, oft got without merit and lost without deserving. You have lost no reputation at all, unless you repute yourself a loser.[5]

It is true that reputations are often undeserved, for bad or for good. But Iago carries this too far. His cynicism is all-consuming.

Declaring oneself against evil, of which Iago could be literature's greatest representation, is an easy moral choice, and thus not a central concern of tragedy. Tragedy can be about the decision to confront or not to confront evil when other considerations, equally grave, are in play. Fighting evil is a good, but it is also a good not to overextend your political and military capacities in the service of fighting it. And that could mean putting up with a certain amount of evil. Individuals, such as writers and intellectuals, are free to declare against evil. Statesmen have to be careful not to promise too much. Vladimir Putin, however cynical and criminal, is still not Stalin, whose crimes vastly overshadow his. Yet it was Stalin with whom Franklin Roosevelt formed an alliance, as the United States supplied the Soviet Union with $11.3 billion in materiel through the Lend-Lease Act. And that World War II alliance achieved the good of defeating Hitler. That is another aspect of the battle of good against good. Henry Kissinger wrote as a young man that, "Every statesman

---

must attempt to reconcile what is considered just with what is considered possible."[6] What is just involves the moral values of a statesman's own society, while what is possible involves the values and domestic situations of other societies with which he must deal.

For example:

Saddam Hussein, who killed hundreds of thousands of people beyond initiating the Iran-Iraq War, accomplished far more evil than Shakespeare's Iago. But ending his evil, as the younger Bush administration decided to do by toppling his regime, led to even more civilian suffering, as well as to other awful consequences, because of the nature and situation of Iraqi society. That is the stuff of tragedy, which inheres at its most extreme and most exalted in the kind of narrow, fateful, binary choices the younger Bush had to make.

And President Joe Biden, as well as his successors, may have to make other fateful, binary choices regarding other leaders morally beyond the pale, such as Putin, or China's Xi Jinping. Remember that Nixon and Kissinger formed a truce with China, even as the depredations of the Cultural Revolution were still in progress, in order to balance against the Soviet Union, and even as they achieved détente with the latter. This accomplished the highest moral goal of the Cold War, to keep it from going *hot* through a favorable balance of power. Again, the battle of good versus good means accepting a certain amount of evil. Righteousness, however morally satisfying, can be the enemy of wise statecraft.

Obviously, tragedy inheres in our characters. If there were no evil people in this world, there would be no hard choices about how to confront them. But the good and prideful can come to tragic ends by merely standing up for what they conceive as their honor. When Sophocles' Ajax, the great soldier and man of action, is denied by his fellow Greeks the armor of the dead Achilles — it is given to the wily and less deserving Odysseus instead — Ajax feels himself humiliated: afterward, for utterly no reason, he kills a herd of cattle while in a trance. He then comes to his senses and out of shame commits suicide on his own sword.

We have seen how pride makes men blind and leads them to make tragic choices, but Ajax's excessive pride and sense of honor are directed only at himself. Just as pride can lead to self-delusion, it can also be intertwined with excessive feelings of guilt and humiliation. Thus pride is crucial to tragedy.

The weight of tragedy may be heaviest on King Lear, who is a far more profoundly developed character than Ajax, reflecting the distance tragedy has traveled from the ancient Greeks to Shakespeare. Bearing the dead Cordelia in his arms, the daughter whose loyalty he did not recognize until it was too late, he exclaims,

> Howl, howl, howl! O, (you) are men of stones!
> Had I your tongues and eyes, I'd use them so
> That heaven's vault should crack. She's gone
> Forever.[7]

But as awful as this is — a family tragedy is the most tragic of all — tragedy still has a deeper and final dimension: time itself.

Chapter 14

TIME IS UNGRATEFUL

Having lived in Greece for seven years and having traveled throughout the Eastern Orthodox world — a world that preserves through Byzantium much of the heritage of ancient Greece — I know that *aletheia,* a word I will always associate with the Orthodox Easter service, carries a special emotional charge. It means "truth." "Christ has risen, *aletheia* (in truth) he has risen." But it also has a deeper, ancient meaning. *Aletheia* literally means *not* forgetting, or *not* forgotten. And what is not forgotten, not consigned to oblivion, are the great deeds of heroic warriors.[1] This effort is necessary because so many actions that are worth preserving are in fact forgotten. Time is ungrateful to much that is valiant and noble.

Time, *chronos,* exposes tragic heroes most dangerously. The merely successful among us, defined by our worldly compromises, have few pretensions about being remembered for long.[2] But the hero, out of honor, will not accede to folly and therefore doesn't care what the crowd thinks.[3] He has only immortality to hope for, and that can be a lost hope. As Ajax declares,

> Great, unfathomable time
> Brings dark things into the light
> and buries the bright in darkness.

The chorus responds to Ajax's oration,

> Time truly is great, it quenches all things . . .[4]

It is precisely because everything passes, and so much is forgotten, that we must learn humility. With humility come salvation and, equally important, moderation.

Time has nothing to offer us but oblivion. It cannot induce good behavior, or even consequences for bad behavior. It is precisely because all is practically forgotten that we are free to act with abandon.

Thus it is only fear and shame that discipline us.

Again, hear Sophocles in *Ajax:*

> Where fear and shame come together
> in a man, they act to preserve him. . . . Fear
> is the cornerstone of all order.[5]

Because fear and shame are the basis of order, and therefore ultimately of civilization itself, men, aside from the outright evil, are full of remorse.

Orestes weeps "for all things done . . . for the whole race," and for his "own fate." Though his lamentation is specifically for the murder of his mother and her lover, he also speaks for all time. As the Chorus replies: "No man upon earth shall be brought to the end/Of his days unwounded by sorrow."[6]

This is all very bleak, I know.

Because it is bleak, and because except for the true believers among us there is nothing beyond the grave, the only redemption in this world is through love: the almost religious devotion to other human beings; to feel their pain and sorrow and joy and gladness as you do your own. Love is all that exists when everything else is scraped away. Nostalgia is a function of love and the good memories that arise from it. Shakespeare telescopes all this in *Antony and Cleopatra*. As Antony dies, Cleopatra laments,

> . . . there is nothing left remarkable
> Beneath the visiting moon.[7]

The movements of armies, the passing of historical ages, the pendulum of geopolitics — all are affected by Antony's death, and yet they do not outweigh a great love. With Antony gone, the world and history itself end for the Queen of Egypt.

And love is interwoven with reconciliation. Without the former, the latter cannot exist. Reconciliation is the final note of Aeschylus's *The Oresteia* and Sophocles' *Ajax*. Orestes is forgiven and the Eumenides are persuaded to give up their vengeance. Odysseus resolves to give his former enemy, Ajax, a proper burial. Love and reconciliation are allowed to flourish inside a world order sustained by fear and shame.

Here is Camus:

> Promethean men, without flinching from their difficult
> calling, will keep watch over the earth and the tireless grass. In
> the thunder and lightning of the gods, the chained hero keeps
> his quiet faith in man.[8]

Men and women will reconcile their struggle for survival with the need to do good amid their own starkly limited choices. To reduce all actions to the need for survival is lowering, but to dismiss survival altogether and be concerned only with the greater good is to take survival for granted. That is a luxury not given to most of us, or to most nations.

So the labor of life goes on . . .

And what is ultimately wrought is, for me, best manifested in the paintings of Velázquez and Goya, the two geniuses of Spain's great micro-civilization.

Here is an art of distance, softening an otherwise cruel objectivity while celebrating the raw, earthen intensity of life. It is a noble art, and translates myth into everyday terms. Because it is released from classicism, it is also released from perfectionism. It accepts the trials and limitations of existence. There inheres in this work a dignified gravity of analysis and truth — ravenous truth — all set against the backdrop of a world that is insecure.[9]

Tragedy, on which all realism is based, is less a theory than a sensibility.

EPILOGUE

History counsels prudence. Which means leadership and decision-making are all about personal character. Since we are not angels, ambition is also useful. George H. W. Bush was a fiercely ambitious man who continually sought appointed and elected positions and who fought a dirty presidential campaign against Michael Dukakis in 1988. Yet upon his election as president, he made one wise and momentous foreign policy decision after another, all of which emphasized a respect for tragic limits. He temporarily cooled ties with China after the Tiananmen massacre but did not break diplomatic relations with Beijing, as journalists and intellectuals were then demanding. His administration deliberately went into quiet mode upon the collapse of communist regimes in Eastern Europe so as not to provoke a Soviet military response, again leaving journalists and intellectuals dissatisfied. He ejected Iraqi forces from Kuwait but he did so without pushing toward Baghdad. The elder Bush, an authentic World War II hero, had character when and where it counted. He was the last American president to embrace the use of military power while thinking carefully and tragically about it. He was our last aristocrat in the White House, the last spiritual descendant of Eisenhower.

Oddly enough, it was a moment of public embarrassment for Bush that illuminates his wise sensibility for me. During a visit to Ukraine shortly before the collapse of the Soviet Union, Bush delivered a speech in Kiev on August 1, 1991, in which he warned of "suicidal nationalism." The phrase as well as the speech itself worked to undermine the Ukrainian struggle for independence. This caused *New York Times* columnist William Safire to label Bush's address his "Chicken Kiev speech," after a dish of stuffed chicken breast, for its exceedingly weak tone. Safire thought Bush's words constituted a "colossal misjudgment" of the Soviet and Ukrainian situation.[1] But was it? The weakening and collapse of the Soviet Union led to internecine ethnic and nationalist wars in the Caucasus and parts of Central Asia. As for Ukraine, precisely because of geography, history, and language, it will always matter more to Moscow than to Washington, and therefore its independence remains a flashpoint among the great powers. Nationalism in the former Soviet Union helped produce Vladimir Putin, a bitterer adversary of the West than the last Soviet premier, Mikhail Gorbachev, ever was. Though Bush's words certainly did not fit the mood of the moment, his inherent caution and warning against a suicidal nationalistic age beyond the Cold War demonstrated a greater wisdom, given Putin's later actions. Safire, meanwhile, would go on to become a prominent champion of the Iraq War.

Since the 1991 Gulf War, with the elder Bush as the commander in chief, we have had, with the exception of the Balkans, a string of misbegotten military adventures. The Balkan interventions came after the end of the Cold War but before 9/11, and before China began rapidly building a great navy—turning our eyes firmly toward the Pacific. The United States sent troops into the Balkans mainly for a humanitarian purpose, and mainly because it had the luxury to do so, as there was no obvious strategic competitor then on the horizon. The Balkans are therefore not an especially good guide for the difficult choices about war and peace we may soon face.

Afghanistan and Iraq are more significant. We live in the shadow of those failures until something else happens that replaces them as an obsession and guidepost. And something else will happen for which the lessons of Afghanistan and Iraq may not prove altogether helpful. History rarely repeats and usually doesn't even rhyme, despite the line often misattributed to Mark Twain. Moreover, it is common to overlearn a lesson. Guilt over the vast human carnage of World War I helped lead to an atmosphere of defeat and appeasement in Great Britain just as Nazi Germany was beginning its rise to power. No one in England wanted to repeat World War I, just as no one now wants to repeat Afghanistan and Iraq, and just as no one wanted to repeat Vietnam through the end of the twentieth century. And yet every villain is not Hitler and every year is not 1939. Decisions by their nature are difficult, and we will face extremely close calls without a neat historical analogy to fall back on.

This will especially be the case in a new age of great power rivalry because of the way that global financial markets, the transfer of vast hydrocarbon resources across seas and continents, and the buildup of terrifying precision-guided weaponry and cyber capabilities are interwoven. Never before has thinking tragically — and husbanding fear without being immobilized by it — been more necessary. Passion should not be allowed to distort analysis, even as social media does exactly that.

In this effort, the literary classics will ultimately be firmer and more useful guides than any social science methodology for those who have not had a personal experience with war and death.

—

NOTES

PREFACE

1. Albert Hourani, *A History of the Arab Peoples* (Cambridge, Mass.: Harvard University Press, 1991 and 2002), p. 144.

CHAPTER 1. THE BATTLE OF GOOD AGAINST GOOD

1. Harold Bloom, *Shakespeare: The Invention of the Human* (New York: Riverhead Books, 1998), pp. 388–89 and 404.

2. John D. Rosenberg, Introduction to Thomas Carlyle, *The French Revolution: A History* (New York: The Modern Library, [1837] 2002), p. xviii.

3. Herodotus, *The History*, 9:16, translated by David Grene (Chicago: University of Chicago Press, 1987).

4. Aubrey de Selincourt, *The World of Herodotus* (Boston: Little, Brown, 1962), p. 57.

5. Arthur Schopenhauer, *Essays and Aphorisms,* translated by R. J. Hollingdale (New York: Penguin Books, [1851] 1970 and 2004), p. 164.

6. Maurice Bowra, *Sophoclean Tragedy* (Oxford, UK: The Clarendon Press, [1944] 1965), pp. 175–76.

7. Friedrich Nietzsche, *The Birth of Tragedy,* translated by Douglas Smith (New York: Oxford University Press, [1872] 2000), p. 44.

8. F. L. Lucas, *Greek Tragedy and Comedy* (New York: The Viking Press, [1954] 1968), pp. 6 and 7. Georg Wilhelm Friedrich Hegel, *On Tragedy,* edited by Anne and Henry Paolucci and translated by F. P. B. Osmaston (New York: Harper TorchBooks, [1835] 1962), pp. 99–100.

9. Hegel, *On Tragedy,* translated by T. M. Knox ([1820] 1942), p. 237.

10. This is in some sense a simplification. Albert Camus writes that after the Greeks, the second flourishing of tragedy occurred not only with Shakespeare, but

---

117

a bit more generally with "the countries bordering the edge of western Europe," to include the Elizabethan theater, as well as the Spanish theater of the Golden Age and French seventeenth-century tragedy, which were all nearly contemporaneous. Albert Camus, "On the Future of Tragedy," in *Lyrical and Critical Essays*, edited by Philip Thody and translated from the French by Ellen Conroy Kennedy (New York: Vintage, 1968), p. 296.

11. Schopenhauer, *Essays and Aphorisms*, p. 41.

12. Edith Hamilton, *The Greek Way* (New York: Norton, [1930] 1993), pp. 138–41. Lucas, *Greek Tragedy and Comedy*, p. 30.

13. Lucas, *Greek Tragedy and Comedy*, p. 4.

14. Albert Camus, *The Myth of Sisyphus and Other Essays*, translated from the French by Justin O'Brien (New York: Vintage, [1955] 1991), p. 93.

15. Hans Morgenthau, *Politics Among Nations: The Struggle for Power and Peace*, revised by Kenneth W. Thompson and W. David Clinton (New York: McGraw Hill, [1948] 2006), p. 3.

16. Hamilton, *The Greek Way*, p. 147.

17. *The Federalist*, "McLean edition," 1788.

18. Lucas, *Greek Tragedy and Comedy*, pp. 4–5. Nietzsche, *The Birth of Tragedy*, p. 51.

19. Robert D. Kaplan, *Warrior Politics: Why Leadership Demands a Pagan Ethos* (New York: Random House, 2002), p. 18.

20. Charles Segal, *Tragedy and Civilization: An Interpretation of Sophocles* (Norman: University of Oklahoma Press, [1981] 1999), p. 42.

21. Rosenberg, Introduction to Carlyle, *The French Revolution*, p. xix.

22. Paul A. Cantor, "Tragedy vs. Tyranny," *Wall Street Journal*, February 11–12, 2017, p. C7.

23. Miguel de Unamuno, *Tragic Sense of Life*, translated by J. E. Crawford Flitch (New York: SophiaOmni, [1912] 2014), p. 89. Gustave Flaubert, *Correspondance, troisième série (1854–1869)* (Paris, 1910).

24. Leslie Mitchell, *Maurice Bowra: A Life* (New York: Oxford University Press, 2009), pp. 33, 37–38, and 209.

25. Bowra, *Sophoclean Tragedy*, pp. 358–60 and 367.

26. A. C. Bradley, "Hegel's Theory of Tragedy," 1950, in Hegel, *On Tragedy*, edited by Paolucci, p. 369.

CHAPTER 2. THE AGE OF DIONYSUS

1. Tony Tanner, Introduction to William Shakespeare, *Tragedies, Volume 2* (New York: Everyman's Library, 1993), pp. cx–cxi.

2. Segal, *Tragedy and Civilization*, pp. 43 and 206.

3. Conrad, the Pole, intensely disliked the Russianness of Dostoevsky, particularly as demonstrated in *Crime and Punishment*. And *Under Western Eyes* was partly intended as an answer to Dostoevsky's novel. But I find this all somewhat ironic, given the similar, overarching sensibilities in both works.

4. Nietzsche, *The Birth of Tragedy*, p. 51. Richard Rutherford, Introduction to *Euripides: The Bacchae and Other Plays*, translated by John Davie (New York: Penguin Books, 2005), pp. viii and x.

5. William Shakespeare, *The Tragedy of Hamlet, Prince of Denmark*, Act 5, scene 2, lines 403 and 422–27.

6. Tanner, Introduction to Shakespeare, *Tragedies, Volume 2*, p. xv.

7. Segal, *Tragedy and Civilization*, pp. 2 and 42.

8. Nietzsche, *The Birth of Tragedy*, pp. 19 and 22–23.

9. N. T. Croally, *Euripidean Polemic: The Trojan Women and the Function of Tragedy* (New York: Cambridge University Press, 1994), pp. 69 and 257–58.

10. Rutherford, Introduction to Davie's translations of *Euripides*, pp. xxvii–xxviii and xxxii.

11. Lucas, *Greek Tragedy and Comedy*, p. 298.

12. Euripides, *The Trojan Women*, translated by F. L. Lucas, lines 1136–38 in F. L. Lucas, *Greek Drama for Everyman* (J. M. Dent, 1954); reissued as *Greek Tragedy and Comedy* (Viking/Compass, 1973).

13. Rutherford, *Euripides*, p. 122.

14. In E. M. Forster's *The Longest Journey*, a schoolmaster comes upon Dionysian power and is horrified. "He approved of a little healthy roughness, but this was pure brutality. What had come over his boys? Were they not gentlemen's sons? He would not admit that if you herd together human beings before they can understand each other the great god Pan is angry, and will in the end evade your regulations and drive them mad." (Middlesex, England: Penguin Books, [1907] 1975), p. 189.

15. Lucas, *Greek Tragedy and Comedy*, p. 235.

16. Robert Graves, *The Greek Myths: Volume One* (New York: Penguin Books, [1955] 1981), pp. 104–5. Edith Hamilton, *Mythology: Timeless Tales of Gods and Heroes* (Boston: Little, Brown, [1942] 2011), pp. 65, and 67–68. Rutherford, Introduction to Davie's translations of *Euripides*, p. xxxix.

17. Euripides, *The Bacchae*, translated by F. L. Lucas, lines 17–20 and 40–41, in F. L. Lucas, *Greek Drama for Everyman* (J. M. Dent, 1954); reissued as *Greek Tragedy and Comedy* (Viking/Compass, 1973).

18. Euripides, *The Bacchae*, lines 281–85.

19. Euripides, *The Bacchae*, lines 1122–27.

20. Euripides, *The Bacchae*, lines 1249–50.

21. Euripides, *The Bacchae*, lines 300–314.

22. Euripides, *The Bacchae*, line 1390.

23. Amitav Ghosh, *The Great Derangement: Climate Change and the Unthinkable* (Chicago: University of Chicago Press, 2016), pp. 21–22 and 35–36.

24. Henry James, *The Princess Casamassima* (New York: Penguin Books, [1886] 1987), pp. 330 and 583.

25. Fyodor Dostoevsky, *Demons* (formerly translated as *The Possessed*), new translation by Richard Pevear and Larissa Volokhonsky (New York: Vintage, [1872] 1994), p. 251.

26. George Steiner, *Tolstoy or Dostoevsky: An Essay in the Old Criticism* (New Haven, Conn.: Yale University Press, 1959 and 1996), pp. 40, 188–89, and 209.

CHAPTER 3. ORDER: THE ULTIMATE NECESSITY

1. Richard Seaford, Introduction to Aeschylus, *The Oresteia: Agamemnon, Choephoroe, Eumenides* (New York: Everyman's Library, 2004), p. xiii.

2. Seaford, Introduction to Aeschylus, *The Oresteia*, p. xiii.

3. Segal, *Tragedy and Civilization*, p. 30.

4. Sigmund Freud, *Civilization and Its Discontents*, translated from the German by Joan Riviere (Garden City, N.Y.: Doubleday, 1930), pp. 61–62.

5. The medieval theologian Abu Hamid Ghazali famously said much the same thing.

6. Albert Camus, *The Rebel: An Essay on Man in Revolt*, translated from the French by Anthony Bower (New York: Vintage International, [1951] 1991), p. 21.

7. Tanner, Introduction to Shakespeare, *Tragedies, Volume 2*, p. xlv.

8. Lucas, *Greek Tragedy and Comedy*, p. 17.

9. Rutherford, Introduction to Davie's translations of *Euripides*, p. xv.

10. Lucas, *Greek Tragedy and Comedy*, p. 109. Aeschylus, *The Oresteia: Agamemnon, Choephoroe, Eumenides*, translated by George Thomson (New York: Everyman's Library, 2004), p. 91, lines 1046–48.

11. Bloom, *Shakespeare*, pp. 77–78.

12. William Shakespeare, *Titus Andronicus*, Act 1, scene 1, line 55.

13. Joseph Conrad, *Under Western Eyes* (Garden City, N.Y.: Doubleday, Page, and Company, 1924), Author's Note, p. x.

14. George Steiner, *The Death of Tragedy* (New Haven, Conn.: Yale University Press, [1961] 1980), p. 167.

15. Anthony Trollope, *Phineas Finn* (New York: Everyman's Library, [1869] 2001), pp. 174 and 258.

16. Camus, *The Rebel*, pp. 23 and 25.

17. Albert Camus, *Lyrical and Critical Essays*, edited by Philip Thody and translated from the French by Ellen Conroy Kennedy (New York: Vintage Books, 1968), pp. 291–92.

18. Herman Melville, *Billy Budd, Sailor (An Inside Narrative)*, included in *Billy Budd, Sailor and Other Stories* (New York: Penguin Books, [1924] 1986), pp. 350, 352, 361, and 364.

19. Melville, *Billy Budd*, pp. 361–62.

20. Camus, *Lyrical and Critical Essays*, pp. 301–2.

CHAPTER 4. ORDER AND NECESSITY MUST BE OBEYED, EVEN WHEN THEY ARE UNJUST

1. Nietzsche, *The Birth of Tragedy*, pp. vii, 60, and 111.

2. Hegel, *On Tragedy*, edited by Paolucci, pp. 47, 325, and 369. Aeschylus, *Agamemnon*, translated by F. L. Lucas, line 218, in F. L. Lucas, *Greek Drama for Everyman* (J. M. Dent, 1954); reissued as *Greek Tragedy and Comedy* (Viking/Compass, 1973). William Shakespeare, *The Tragedy of King Lear*, Act 4, scene 3, lines 37–38.

3. Bowra, *Sophoclean Tragedy*, p. 209.

4. Bowra, *Sophoclean Tragedy*, pp. 61, 366, and 374.

5. Schopenhauer, *Essays and Aphorisms*, p. 168.

CHAPTER 5. ORDER CREATES PERPETUAL CONFLICT BETWEEN LOYALTY TO THE FAMILY AND LOYALTY TO THE STATE

1. Garry Wills, *Saint Augustine* (New York: Viking, 1999), p. 119. Ernest Gellner, *Muslim Society* (New York: Cambridge University Press, 1981), pp. 20, 24–26, and 33.

2. Georg Wilhelm Friedrich Hegel, *The Philosophy of Fine Art* (London: Osmaton, 1920), p. 324.

3. Paul Cantor, *Shakespeare's Roman Trilogy: The Twilight of the Ancient World* (Chicago: University of Chicago Press, 2017), p. 84.

4. Bowra, *Sophoclean Tragedy*, p. 64.

5. Sophocles, *Antigone*, translated by F. L. Lucas, lines 672–78, in F. L. Lucas, *Greek Drama for Everyman* (J. M. Dent, 1954); reissued as *Greek Tragedy and Comedy* (Viking/Compass, 1973).

6. Sophocles, *Antigone*, lines 929–30.

7. Bowra, *Sophoclean Tragedy*, p. 99.

8. Segal, *Tragedy and Civilization*, pp. 186 and 190.

9. Euripides, *Iphigenia at Aulis*, translated by John Davie, lines 397–401.

10. Euripides, *Iphigenia at Aulis*, lines 1258–69.

11. Euripides, *Iphigenia at Aulis*, line 1353.

12. Euripides, *Iphigenia at Aulis*, line 1364.

13. Euripides, *Iphigenia at Aulis,* lines 1374–91.
14. William Shakespeare, *Coriolanus,* Act 1, scene 3, lines 3–4.
15. Shakespeare, *Coriolanus,* Act 1, scene 3, lines 25–27.
16. Cantor, *Shakespeare's Roman Trilogy,* p. 135. Bloom, *Shakespeare,* p. 580.

CHAPTER 6. THE STATE BECOMES
THE WELLSPRING OF AMBITION

1. Euripides, *Iphigenia at Aulis,* lines 517–20.
2. Bowra, *Sophoclean Tragedy,* p. 374.
3. William Shakespeare, *The Tragedy of Julius Caesar,* Act 2, scene 1, lines 21–26.
4. Shakespeare, *Julius Caesar,* Act 1, scene 2, lines 192–93.
5. Shakespeare, *Julius Caesar,* Act 1, scene 2, lines 142–45.
6. Sophocles, *Philoctetes,* translated by Carl Phillips (New York: Oxford University Press, 2003), lines 1165–70.
7. Bloom, *Shakespeare,* pp. xix and 17.
8. William Shakespeare, *The Tragedy of Hamlet, Prince of Denmark,* Act 3, scene 1, lines 91–97.
9. Shakespeare, *Julius Caesar,* Act 2, scene 1, lines 66–72.
10. William Shakespeare, *The Tragedy of Macbeth,* Act 1, scene 5, lines 48–50.
11. Steiner, *The Death of Tragedy,* p. 128.
12. Shakespeare, *Julius Caesar,* Act 3, scene 1, lines 300–301.

CHAPTER 7. AMBITION AND THE STRUGGLE
AGAINST TYRANNY AND INJUSTICE

1. Aeschylus, *Prometheus Bound,* translated by F. L. Lucas, lines 105–8, 500, 611, and 1021, F. L. Lucas, *Greek Drama for Everyman* (J. M. Dent, 1954); reissued as *Greek Tragedy and Comedy* (Viking/Compass, 1973).
2. Aeschylus, *Prometheus Bound,* lines 406–8.
3. Hamilton, *Mythology,* pp. 92–93.
4. Camus, *The Rebel,* p. 240.
5. Robert Browning, *Pauline: A Fragment of a Confession* (1833).
6. Leo Strauss, *On Tyranny: Including the Strauss-Kojève Correspondence,* edited by Victor Gourevitch and Michael S. Roth (Chicago: University of Chicago Press, 1961), p. 45. Strauss is referring to Xenophon's dialogue between Hiero, tyrant of Syracuse, and Simonides, a wise poet.
7. Sophocles, *Antigone,* translated by David Grene, lines 393–95.

---

8. Shakespeare, *Hamlet,* Act 5, scene 1, lines 77–78 and 216–19.

9. Schopenhauer, *Essays and Aphorisms,* p. 42.

CHAPTER 8. WAR AND ITS HORRORS

1. Aeschylus, *Agamemnon,* translated by Lucas, lines 556–61.

2. William Shakespeare, *Henry IV, Part 1,* Act 5, scene 1, lines 131–37.

3. Lucas, *Greek Tragedy and Comedy,* p. 236.

4. Lucas, *Greek Tragedy and Comedy,* pp. 294–95.

5. Euripides, *Trojan Women,* translated by Alan Shapiro (New York: Oxford University Press, 2009), lines 209–16.

6. Euripides, *Trojan Women,* lines 431–39 and 464.

7. Euripides, *Trojan Women,* lines 427–28.

8. Euripides, *Trojan Women,* lines 877–78.

9. Euripides, *Trojan Women,* lines 1472–73.

10. Euripides, *Trojan Women,* line 1575.

11. T. S. Eliot, *Selected Essays* (London: Faber and Faber, 1932), p. 131.

CHAPTER 9. BECAUSE WAR IS EVER-PRESENT, THE BURDEN OF POWER IS OVERWHELMING

1. Shakespeare, *Julius Caesar,* Act 2, scene 2, lines 32–33.

2. Aeschylus, *Choephoros,* line 901.

3. Euripides, *Iphigenia at Aulis,* lines 680–81.

4. Euripides, *Iphigenia at Aulis,* lines 447–48.

5. Bloom, *Shakespeare,* pp. 249–50 and 263.

6. Shakespeare, *King Lear,* Act 1, scene 1, lines 339–40.

7. Aeschylus, *Persians,* translated by Janet Lembke and C. John Herington; introduction by C. John Herington (New York: Oxford University Press, 1981), p. 9.

8. Herington, Introduction to Aeschylus, *Persians,* p. 26.

9. Aeschylus, *Persians,* lines 81–83.

10. Aeschylus, *Persians,* line 126.

11. Aeschylus, *Persians,* lines 442–45.

12. Aeschylus, *Persians,* lines 567–70.

13. Aeschylus, *Persians,* lines 751 and 893.

14. Aeschylus, *Persians,* line 900.

15. Aeschylus, *Persians,* lines 1054–66.

16. Aeschylus, *Persians,* lines 1357–58.

CHAPTER 10. IMPERIAL WARS ARE DECIDED BY FATE

1. Cantor, *Shakespeare's Roman Trilogy*, pp. 60–62 and 83.

2. Bloom, *Shakespeare*, p. 556. Tanner, Introduction to Shakespeare, *Tragedies, Volume 2*, p. lxxii. William Shakespeare, *The Tragedy of Antony and Cleopatra*, Act 1, scene 4, line 10.

3. C. P. Cavafy, "The God Abandons Antony" (1911) in *Collected Poems*, translated by Edmund Keeley and Philip Sherrard and edited by George Savidis (Princeton, N.J.: Princeton University Press, 1975), p. 32. Republished with permission of Princeton University; permission conveyed through Copyright Center Clearance, Inc.

4. Reinhold Niebuhr, *The Irony of American History* (Chicago: University of Chicago Press, 1952), p. 74.

5. Aubrey de Selincourt, *The World of Herodotus* (Boston: Little, Brown, 1962), p. 57.

6. Steiner, *Tolstoy or Dostoevsky*, p. 79.

7. Bowra, *Sophoclean Tragedy*, p. 305.

8. Bowra, *Sophoclean Tragedy*, p. 27.

9. Aeschylus, *Choephoroe*, lines 305–7.

10. Giuseppe Tomasi di Lampedusa, *The Leopard*, translated from the Italian by Archibald Colquhoun (New York: Everyman's Library, [1958] 1998), pp. 52, 132–35, and 164.

CHAPTER 11. FROM THE SUFFERING OF HEROES
COMES THE ESSENCE OF TRAGEDY

1. Bowra, *Sophoclean Tragedy*, p. 368.

2. Segal, *Tragedy and Civilization*, p. 207.

3. Sophocles, *Oedipus at Colonus*, translated by F. L. Lucas, line 1620, in F. L. Lucas, *Greek Drama for Everyman* (J. M. Dent, 1954); reissued as *Greek Tragedy and Comedy* (Viking/Compass, 1973).

4. Sophocles, *Ajax*, translated by Herbert Golder and Richard Pevear (New York: Oxford University Press, 1999), line 178.

5. Shakespeare, *Hamlet*, Act 3, scene 2, lines 234–36.

6. Schopenhauer, *Essays and Aphorisms*, pp. 46–47 and 49.

7. William Wordsworth, *The Borderers*, 1795–97, lines 1 and 5.

8. Sophocles, *Oedipus at Colonus*, translated by David Grene, line 7.

9. Bradley, "Hegel's Theory of Tragedy," p. 370.

10. Bloom, *Shakespeare*, p. 587.

11. Tanner, Introduction to Shakespeare, *Tragedies, Volume 2*, p. lxxvi.

12. Dostoevsky, *Crime and Punishment,* translated by Richard Pevear and Larissa Volokhonsky, pp. 549–50.

CHAPTER 12. THE TRUTH IS POSSESSED
ONLY BY THE OLD AND THE BLIND

1. Sophocles, *Oedipus the King,* translated by F. L. Lucas, line 356, in F. L. Lucas, *Greek Drama for Everyman* (J. M. Dent, 1954); reissued as *Greek Tragedy and Comedy* (Viking/Compass, 1973).

2. Charles Segal, Introduction to Sophocles, *The Theban Plays* (New York: Everyman's Library, 1994), p. xxiii.

3. Aleksandr Solzhenitsyn, *November 1916: The Red Wheel/Knot II,* translated by H. T. Willetts (New York: Farrar, Straus and Giroux, [1984] 1999), p. 337.

4. Bowra, *Sophoclean Tragedy,* p. 354.

5. Sophocles, *Oedipus the King,* lines 1528–30.

6. Sophocles, *Ajax,* lines 153–60.

7. Herodotus, *The History,* 1:32

8. Lionel Trilling, "A Speech on Robert Frost: A Cultural Episode" (1959), in Trilling's *The Moral Obligation to Be Intelligent: Selected Essays,* edited and with an introduction by Leon Wieseltier (Evanston, Ill.: Northwestern University Press, 2008), p. 380.

CHAPTER 13. BECAUSE DIFFERENT GOODS STRUGGLE
AGAINST EACH OTHER, WE HAVE CONSCIENCES

1. Tanner, Introduction to Shakespeare, *Tragedies, Volume 2,* pp. x–xi.

2. Bloom, *Shakespeare,* p. 404.

3. William Shakespeare, *The Tragedy of Othello, The Moor of Venice,* Act 2, scene 3, lines 371–82.

4. Bloom, *Shakespeare,* pp. 436 and 454.

5. Shakespeare, *Othello,* Act 2, scene 3, lines 286–90.

6. Henry A. Kissinger, *A World Restored: Metternich, Castlereagh and the Problems of Peace, 1812–1822* (Boston: Houghton Mifflin, 1957), p. 5.

7. Shakespeare, *King Lear,* Act 5, scene 3, lines 308–11.

CHAPTER 14. TIME IS UNGRATEFUL

1. Tanner, Introduction to Shakespeare, *Tragedies, Volume 2,* p. cvi.

2. Segal, *Tragedy and Civilization,* p. 378.

3. Jean Racine, *Phèdre,* translated from the French by Ted Hughes (New York: Farrar, Straus and Giroux, 1998), Act I/7.

4. Sophocles, *Ajax,* lines 712–14 and 791.

5. Sophocles, *Ajax,* lines 1204 and 1209–10.

6. Aeschylus, *The Oresteia: Choephoroe,* translated by Thomson, lines 1015–16 and 1018–19.

7. Shakespeare, *Antony and Cleopatra,* Act 4, scene 15, lines 77–78.

8. Camus, "Prometheus in the Underworld" (1947), in *Lyrical and Critical Essays,* edited by Philip Thody and translated from the French by Ellen Conroy Kennedy (New York: Vintage Books, 1968), p. 142.

9. Jonathan Brown, *Velázquez: Painter and Courtier* (New Haven, Conn.: Yale University Press, 1986), pp. vii, 30, 74, 104, 146, and 203. Robert Hughes, *Goya* (New York: Knopf, 2003), p. 124.

EPILOGUE

1. William Safire, "After the Fall," *New York Times,* August 29, 1991.

ACKNOWLEDGMENTS

General inspiration came from the late Charles Hill of Yale, to whose eclectic mind I was exposed at numerous dinners over the decades at Henry Kissinger's weekend house in Kent, Connecticut. Charlie's book *Grand Strategies: Literature, Statecraft, and World Order* (2010) provided a demanding guidepost while I wrote. Actually it was Paul Lettow, a colleague in Washington, who had first suggested that I expand into book-length a phrase I had been using periodically in my essays, *thinking tragically to avoid tragedy.* Elbridge Colby, a military strategist and former Pentagon official, added his assent. Adam Klein, a former clerk at the U.S. Supreme Court, read the book in its early stages and made a number of incisive comments regarding its logic. Jim Thomas and Andrew Krepinevich, both leading defense policy analysts, were wise and good friends during a difficult period for me. Thanks also are due to Carol "Rollie" Flynn of the Foreign Policy Research Institute and Richard Fontaine of the Center for a New American Security, whose organizations sustained me while I wrote and completed this book.

Henry Thayer, my literary agent, steered this book to William Frucht at Yale University Press, who would emerge as a memorable editor, combining literary sensitivity, organizational insight, and analytical judgment. Elizabeth M. Lockyer, my assistant, handled the permissions, which sometimes required prodigious detective work. Maria Cabral, my wife of four decades, supplied the love and understanding.

Finally, I thank the editors of *The New Criterion*, who published an earlier version of a portion of Chapter 1: Robert D. Kaplan, "The Tragic Sensibility," *The New Criterion* (May 2017).

Permission is gratefully acknowledged to reproduce excerpts from the following works:

Aeschylus, *Persians*, translated by Janet Lembke and C. J. Herington; introduction by C. J. Herington (New York: Oxford University Press, 1981). Copyright © 1981 by Janet Lembke and C. J. Herington. Reproduced with permission of the Licensor through PLSclear.

From *The Bacchae and Other Plays* by Euripides, translated by John Davie with notes by Richard Rutherford, published by Penguin Classics. Translation copyright © 2005 John Davie. Introduction and editorial material copyright © 2005 Richard Rutherford. All rights reserved. Reprinted by permission of Penguin Books Limited.

Euripides, *Trojan Women*, translated by Alan Shapiro (New York: Oxford University Press, 2009). Copyright © 2009 by Oxford University Press, Inc. Reproduced with permission of the Licensor through PLSclear.

F. L. Lucas, *Greek Drama for Everyman* (J. M. Dent, 1954); reissued as *Greek Tragedy and Comedy* (Viking/Compass, 1973). Reprinted by permission of Dr. S. O. Lucas.

Sophocles, *Ajax*, translated by Herbert Golder and Richard Pevear (New York: Oxford University Press, 1999). Copyright © 2009 by Herbert Golder and Richard Pevear. Reproduced with permission of the Licensor through PLSclear.

—

INDEX

INDEX

INDEX

INDEX